ASCENDING
DAVOS

D0823969

PRAISE FOR *ASCENDING DAVOS*

"The breadth of Meghan FitzGerald's experience in healthcare and her preference for disruptive honesty makes this book a must read for aspiring and current healthcare leaders."

—SENATOR J. ROBERT KERREY

Governor of Nebraska (1983–1987) and US Senator (1989–2001);
Lead Director, Tenet Healthcare;
Managing Director, Allen & Company

"Meghan FitzGerald's personal narrative through American healthcare's corporate corridors—with her occasional yet inevitable stumbles and struggles—provides valuable insight into what it takes to rise above the madding crowd. At the same time she peppers her story with generous and helpful advice to other ambitious leaders planning their ascent up the corporate ladder."

—PETER ARNO

Senior Fellow and Director of Health Policy Research at the
Political Economy Research Institute at UMass-Amherst;
Author of *Against the Odds: The Story of AIDS Drug
Development, Politics and Profits,* nominated for Pulitzer Prize

"The real-deal story of what it takes to compete, succeed, and find meaning in corporate America. Meg's trail blazing is laid out in this book, offering a clear playbook for any young professional looking to rise to the top of America's biggest corporations."

—JASON FRIESEN

Founder and CEO, Trek Medics

"Just read the section on 'The Academic.' Loved it. You have such an engaging writing style, combining important substance with an ability to make the reader feel you're talking directly to her/him."

—MICHAEL SPARER

Professor and Chair in the Department of Health Policy and Management at the Mailman School of Public Health at Columbia University

"Ascending Davos is your 'go-to' guide on how to get &%#@ done. With advice that is rooted in her ascent to the boardroom, Meghan FitzGerald offers practical insights that will allow today's rising stars to become tomorrow's prescient leaders. Whether you are in the middle of your career or just beginning, Meg articulates an intensely personal but practical guide to successfully navigate the corporate labyrinth."

—MARY M. GALLAGHER

Senior Vice President and Chief Marketing Officer, Seniorlink

MEGHAN FITZGERALD

ASCENDING DAVOS

A CAREER JOURNEY FROM THE EMERGENCY ROOM TO THE BOARDROOM

Advantage.

Copyright © 2020 by Meghan FitzGerald.

All rights reserved. No part of this book may be used or reproduced in any manner whatsoever without prior written consent of the author, except as provided by the United States of America copyright law.

Published by Advantage, Charleston, South Carolina.
Member of Advantage Media Group.

ADVANTAGE is a registered trademark, and the Advantage colophon is a trademark of Advantage Media Group, Inc.

Printed in the United States of America.

10 9 8 7 6 5 4 3 2 1

ISBN: 978-1-64225-072-5
LCCN: 2019915823

Cover design by Jamie Wise.
Layout design by George Stevens.

This publication is designed to provide accurate and authoritative information in regard to the subject matter covered. It is sold with the understanding that the publisher is not engaged in rendering legal, accounting, or other professional services. If legal advice or other expert assistance is required, the services of a competent professional person should be sought.

Advantage Media Group is proud to be a part of the Tree Neutral® program. Tree Neutral offsets the number of trees consumed in the production and printing of this book by taking proactive steps such as planting trees in direct proportion to the number of trees used to print books. To learn more about Tree Neutral, please visit **www.treeneutral.com**.

Advantage Media Group is a publisher of business, self-improvement, and professional development books and online learning. We help entrepreneurs, business leaders, and professionals share their Stories, Passion, and Knowledge to help others Learn & Grow. Do you have a manuscript or book idea that you would like us to consider for publishing? Please visit **advantagefamily.com** or call **1.866.775.1696**.

For the hat trick of Mikes in my life—my dad, my brother, and my husband.

CONTENTS

PREFACE xi
Earning a Seat on the Global Stage

SECTION I: THE CAREGIVER 1

CHAPTER 1 3
The First Rung

SECTION II: THE HEALTHCARE EXECUTIVE. 21

CHAPTER 2 23
Stepping Up

CHAPTER 3 43
When It's Working, Then Not

SECTION III: THE ACADEMIC 61

CHAPTER 4 63
Keep Learning

SECTION IV: THE DEALMAKER. 85

CHAPTER 5 87
Reaching the Peak

SECTION V: THE ADVOCATE 105

CHAPTER 6 107
Building "Team Meg"

CHAPTER 7 123
Your Health—Part of the Compensation Package

CONCLUSION 137
Back to Where It All Started

ABOUT THE AUTHOR 143

ACKNOWLEDGMENTS 145

PREFACE

EARNING A SEAT ON THE GLOBAL STAGE

A s I trudged through the icy, mountain streets of Davos, Switzerland, toward the Congress Centre, I began to equate the trek with my ascent from the bedside of patient care to the most elusive halls of power, including this very meeting, which represented a notable apex in my academic, business, and personal achievements. It gave me a moment to reflect on what it took to get here.

For more than twenty years, I had moved through the ranks of healthcare, starting as a nurse providing hands-on care and then moving into the business side of the industry. But it was there at Davos, in the most surreal of places, that I had the opportunity to experience what would represent a global hive of forces surrounding women in the workplace. I was attending the World Economic Forum (WEF), which was on display for the world to watch. Every media outlet from CNBC to the *Daily Mail* is typically on hand at Davos, or DavOOs as it's affectionately known, to cover the who's who of power, money, politics, and decision-making.

The ride to the conference in Davos from Zurich is both stunning and exhilarating: I describe it as a mix of going to college, a once-in-a-lifetime job interview, a few hours in an editorial session of a foreign-policy rag, and a splash of a first date, all blended into a perfectly constructed storm. I almost felt like a member of the UN—until the sound of private helicopters flying overhead reminded me that most of the attendees did not live like the nurse I used to be. I knew I was not part of this club. Instead, I was firmly grounded in public transportation as my means of getting around.

The desire to be everywhere at Davos is overwhelming, and I wanted to make the right impression, especially since this year I was attending as an official member and moderating a few panels. So, I tried to follow the advice given to me by one of the few executive women I knew who attended Davos: "Blend in with a splash of pop." For me, that meant trudging nearly a mile through the snow to the conference center from the lower-ranking hotel with Davos snow cleats attached to my boots and rocking snowboard gear, which was also uber-practical but made me look like an X Games participant.

When an executive is in their zone, usually any thoughts of self-care take a back seat. That happened at Davos; taking care of my health wasn't on the agenda until I was leaving, fever stricken, hacking a brandied lung, and dragging twenty pounds of reading material and business cards back to the Zurich airport. There, I triaged several hundred business cards into piles of "professional, personal, pass," and quickly scribed follow-ups so I wouldn't lose momentum or compete with the other three hundred emails the likes of David Gergen, Marc Benioff, or Pascale Witz would be getting.

At Davos, many of the world problems being discussed with regard to economics, poverty, and health had a head-of-household component, which certainly includes a female aspect. Yet, the lack of women attendees was branded as scandalous, and I found it more than ironic that the very conference that devoted an enormous amount of time, money, and resources to women's health was under-represented in person. While attending Davos the following year, I was mistakenly assumed to be his guest when I showed up anywhere with my husband, a Wall Street macroeconomist and strategist who is widely read on the global markets. He would often respond jokingly and with pride, "Nope, I'm the baggage handler," and would laugh so hard he cried.

At the same time, the subject of the number of women attendees was covered extensively on social media. Some of the press leading up to Davos 2015 asked, "Where are the women?" The Twitter universe alone was losing feathers over the roughly 17 percent women-atten-dance statistic this particular year,[1] followed by dilutive commentary that most of the women there were media, wives, or worse—"a staffer to the stars," the latter being a job that got me where I am today. Still, the statistics found outside of Davos in the halls of power, business, and academic centers aren't much better—and many areas are worse. Note that at Davos 2018, all seven cochairs of the conference were female and they have worked harder than most to incorporate women leaders. On one panel I chaired, one prominent male member refused to participate unless diversity was represented on the panels.

However, as I write this book, women comprise half of the US

---

population. They earn more than half (60 percent) of the undergraduate and master's degrees, nearly half of the law and medical degrees (47 and 48 percent, respectively), and more than one-third of the MBAs (38 percent). They also make up nearly half of the labor force in the US (47 percent), and nearly half of the college-educated labor force (49 percent). Yet, in S&P 500 companies, where they are 44 percent of the workforce, only 25 percent are found in executive and senior-level positions, 20 percent hold board seats, and only 6 percent are in the role of CEO.[2]

These numbers show the reality of what many women will reach at the peak of their corporate climb.

This particular year at Davos, Janet Yellen, then chair of the US Federal Reserve System; Angela Merkel, chancellor of Germany; and Christine Lagarde, then chair of the International Monetary Fund, were probably hands down some of the most powerful humans on the planet, at least to me and my friends on Wall Street. I called them the "trifecta of financial power." And from the quaint tables in the Kaffee Klatsch restaurant to the private suites at the InterContinental Davos, the money world was obsessing on whether Mario Draghi, head of the ECB (Eurozone Central Bank, a job Lagarde holds today) was going to follow Janet Yellen's lead on monetary easing (tech speak for printing money). And Draghi would have a hard time doing this due to fears of inflation. It was clear Lagarde's finesse and Merkel's support ultimately helped him get this done. Why this trifecta of women didn't shut down the internet, or at least the WEF Twitter handle, was bizarre to me.

The woman executive who had advised me on the conference

---

2   Judith Warner and Danielle Corley, "The Women's Leadership Gap," *Center for American Progress*, May 21, 2017, accessed December 4, 2018, https:// www.americanprogress.org/issues/women/reports/2017/05/21/432758/ womens-leadership-gap.

code also advised that I read everything ahead of time so that I could "show up smart." That, I could do. In fact, day one at Davos was awful because I didn't sleep well the night before; I was worrying about the WEF Global Agenda Council on Ageing panel session that I was going to help moderate. It featured the foremost minds in healthcare, policy, academics, medicine, technology, and government. I was filling in for my boss on the panel, so I wanted to be more than prepared—which is the norm for me. Even though some panelists appeared to be confidently and aptly winging it, I was as ready as if it were a dissertation defense.

Having awoken with a migraine from an emerging cold, I gave myself a shot of sumatriptan and proceeded to put up a good show on the panel. I knew there was no way I could call in sick, and so I came through. But at what cost? And there, in Davos, I began to realize that many climb their own career ladder managing stress, family, and life, often with the feeling of an icicle thumping through the eye while earning the fleeting shot to be on the big stage. As I looked back on my career there were probably ten of these high-profile moments, and it always felt like the last one so I never missed.

Throughout my journey, I've evolved my career from one that valued promotions and wealth creation into one that values health and contribution to a larger cause. Today, I have a career that allows me to really do what makes me happy, which includes having a little more freedom to help others. As I write this book, I'm an adjunct associate professor of public health at Columbia University, and I'm working in private equity, helping to invest in new companies and select management teams including CEOs.

Along the way, I learned some valuable principles that I'm sharing with you at the end of each section of this book. These sections represent the various phases of my career. As you read these principles,

I hope you can apply some of what I've learned to your own situation:

- Healthcare like many specialized sectors is about "content and connections." Be overprepared and stay close to movers and shakers in your field. Make it a job.

- Have a long-term strategy for your career ascension, but understand that those plans versus the reality on the ground will require you to adapt using short-term goals.

- Star sponsors pull you up and beyond. And they are likely more often male. Find sponsors early and justify their inclusion of your career with theirs.

- Have a brand and be maniacal about cultivating and promoting it. Mine is Get Shit Done, or GSD.

- Education and training is a constant and the great equalizer, and you should focus on being financially literate personally and professionally. That means more math and time with finance mentors.

- Health is your wealth. Learn that early. Distance yourself from "sick" bosses and companies.

Today, I'm up here on my own peak and doing well, in part, because of lessons, tactics, and principles deployed along the way. Early on in my career, I realized that those at the highest levels of my industry had a mix of "content and connections," and, in order to have the same, I needed to put a premium on training and education. And later in life (but not too late) I made the decision to value health up there with compensation and other life choices and benefits. A career in healthcare should always keep the patient as your focus and that patient may include you or your family. That's a key lesson I learned during my career climb, and a key message I hope you reflect on for yourself as you ascend or glide, no matter where you are today.

My life mantra is, "She who dies with the most stories wins." Remember that your life endeavors will ultimately be a reflection of who you are and what you stood for. Your professional and personal contribution is all that remains and matters.

SECTION I
THE CAREGIVER

CHAPTER 1

THE FIRST RUNG

L ike many leaders, I've found that success is a product of three things: education, experience, and a powerful network. I learned those lessons while working in and around the 18 percent of the US economy that represents healthcare—from the front lines of healthcare delivery, including time on an Indian reservation, to the boardrooms of Fortune 50 healthcare companies.

I grew up as the daughter of parents that worked for the FBI. My mom and dad met and married while in the agency, and Marge, my beloved godmother and my mom's best friend, worked there until she died post-9/11 in New York from lung cancer. She was a nonsmoking, healthy, marathon runner, dedicated to law enforcement and protecting others, which made her death especially tragic. Probably taking after my parents, I was always incredibly curious, always looking around corners—a trait that has served me well over the years.

Over time, I also developed the ability to triage. In medicine, triage means to care for the critical patients and the ones you can save first. Losing my dad at age eighteen forced that triaging process. When the ambulance came to get him, it put me on the road to being an "eminent orphan," a term coined by author Malcolm Gladwell, one of the many come-from-beyond stories in the world that have been driven, in part, by the death of a parent.[3] I knew right then the importance of going to work for money and focusing on what mattered. Sometimes my mom would worry about "going under" financially, but I wasn't waiting to see whether we were actually going to be living in our ugly, wood-paneled, green station wagon. I took a job waitressing four nights a week and diligently counted out my tips when I got home.

In high school, I was a decent student, with the occasional A in science or art. But I knew a track scholarship was waiting for me around the bend, which was my path out of the middle of the pack. At an early age, I instinctively focused on the important events to accelerate my position in life and deemphasized those that had little payoff. My plan was to literally run like hell to make it in life. And I wasn't alone. I was part of a very diverse group of middle-pack track mates, a few who were much worse off than me financially. The best of them, Betty, had a hole in the toe of her sneaker and lived in the worst part of town, yet no one could touch her 200-meter time, no matter how much they spent on their sneakers. That taught me early on that raw talent is a great equalizer—it can't be bought.

After studying prelaw and running track in Washington, DC, I transferred and earned a bachelor of science in nursing from Fairfield

3　Robert Krulwich, "Successful Children Who Lost a Parent—Why Are There So Many of Them?" *NPR*, October 16, 2013, accessed November 9, 2018, https://www.npr.org/sections/krulwich/2013/10/15/234737083/ successful-children-who-lost-a-parent-why-are-there-so-many-of-them.

University. With that degree, I was determined to get the best job that I could, one that offered money and advancement. I've had a lifelong battle with asthma, so I decided to head for Tucson, Arizona—my dad's favorite place on Earth and a warmer climate for my lungs—where there were a lot of job openings at the time. I sold my beloved Volkswagen Rabbit convertible for $7,000—the weird blue color they don't make anymore—packed up a U-Haul, and headed west.

I arrived in Tucson one cold night under the brightest stars I had ever seen. I checked into a Motel 6 on a weekly rate, trying to preserve funds that were down by $1,500 after the cross-country trip. I did need a car, and in a lot near this Motel 6, I bought a lemon of a Honda for $400, which was all I needed at the time.

The motel was not in the best part of town—gunshots rang out the first night of my stay—but I was determined to live below my means. Despite having a nursing degree, I went out the next morning in search of a waitressing job. My nursing license would have to clear state board certification before I could begin working in Arizona, so I planned to wait tables to pay for my living expenses until that came through.

Once it did, I originally planned to work full time in the emergency department at Tucson Medical Center, which was my primary interest and where I got my start in healthcare interning in the ER during nursing school. But with a wide-open job market, I was also offered a job working in a dialysis unit for a company called Gambro Healthcare. To help me decide which job would be my primary focus, I put together a spreadsheet that scored each in the categories of boss, work environment, ability for career growth, and pay. The dialysis job scored highest across the board.

My initial training was technical and fascinating. Learning to remove several pints of blood and clean it in a machine outside the body was a medical miracle that required a mix of care and science. And given the intimacy and time for the procedure, patients became like family members.

In order to receive dialysis, most patients needed a fistula, a large vein in which to administer a wide-gauge (very thick) needle that could process a lot of blood in and out of the body rapidly. Many fistulas were created using a patient's own veins. Some of the fistulas were bovine, and I thought it was interesting to see patients with cow veins bulging out of their arms.

Dialysis usually involved having patients sit in a large circle surrounding a nursing and tech station so their vitals—like blood pressure—facial expressions, and progress could be monitored. Each nurse was responsible for a circle—or pod—of patients. After six weeks of training, I was on my own to care for a pod for three shifts, a total of twelve hours.

The patient "turnovers" were the most intense, with medication administration, removal of needles, and patients who could "crash out" with low blood pressure as a result of fluid removal. But I loved the autonomy of it all. I was in charge of the entire episode of care. The medications, procedures, and protocols were largely standing orders, so unless a physician was rounding, it was all me, supported by a team of intensely dedicated patient-care techs.

Every day was different, but the patients and their chronic-disease progression and protocol-driven care were a constant. Many family members sat with their loved ones during the three-hour procedure and played games or chatted as they now do today with chemotherapy infusions. It was my first introduction to holistic care. End-stage renal disease was their primary illness, but that was shared with other comorbidities such as depression, hypertension, diabetes, and amputations.

To this day, I find dialysis fascinating because it transcends policy, science, chronic disease, and drug innovation—and because it is front and center in the debate about the costs of healthcare. If you wanted to learn about American healthcare in one therapeutic area or disease state, the study of end-stage renal disease and dialysis is a great place to start.

Dialysis has been used since the 1940s and is really one of the first chronic-disease patient groups. Drugs used in dialysis have been some notable biotech blockbusters. Dialysis is where I learned the importance of drug development, as it ushered in a wave of billion-dollar biotech companies.

The field also has a fierce debate and public-health history, from the patent disputes on Epogen (a drug used to combat anemia) between Amgen and several competitors through the years, to the three-state outbreak of hemolysis traced to faulty blood-tubing sets. On the expense front, I think a lot of the buzzwords around episodes of care and payment bundling got their roots in renal disease dating back in 1972, when Medicare benefits were extended to cover end-stage renal disease. And it's interesting to note that one of Europe's first biosimilar drugs (Omnitrope) was approved for use in chronic kidney disease. Recently President Trump signed an executive order aimed at improving medical care for the more than 37 million Americans with kidney disease, including paying the costs of kidney transplants and related care.

I remember my first lunch with a drug representative was an "Epogen lunch." A lovely and bright woman named Beth showed up to talk with us about the product insert for Epoetin Alfa. It was called a clinical "in-service," but most of the attendees came for the free lunch. I admit to being more focused on her cool clinical job and wondered how I could get one. She was a nurse educator who dressed well and spoke even better, and she was passionate about dialysis. I was in a thermal shirt; male scrubs that I cinched around the waist; and ugly, plastic, teal-colored clogs. Her pitch seemed easy, since everyone in dialysis knew a good hematocrit (number and size of red blood cells) was an optimal goal for dialysis patients.

I thought Epogen was like a Honda; anyone could sell it. Why not me? I made a mental note to think about a career in pharma. In the meantime, however, I was close to being promoted to a unit director or clinical lead—unless I blew it.

A STOMACH-TURNING REVERSAL

At this time, patients with severe infections, like MRSA, were kept in isolation and under contact precautions, and patients infected with hepatitis B or C or human immunodeficiency virus (HIV), were largely unknown. Still, healthcare providers must treat all patients equally and without stigma, because bloodborne pathogens can affect anyone—both patients and providers.

Given the intimacy of the dialysis procedure and the size of needles used, an accidental needlestick to the administering health provider would be obvious—not to mention painful. Back then, in nursing, some wrongly considered a needlestick to be more than just embarrassing—it was considered to be an utter failure. In some ways, the needlestick instantaneously turns the nurse into the patient. It's a perverse role reversal that's hard to stomach. I know, because that's exactly what happened to me.

One third shift, while removing one of my patients from a dialysis, I inadvertently jabbed myself with his needle. I'm pretty sure my fishing to recap a dirty needle was the reason. As I stared at my thin latex glove, blood began to pool underneath until the entire finger was red. And my staring at it didn't help the situation: the fear in my face was palpable and obvious to the patient, who asked, "Did you stick yourself?" I lied and said, "No." I was embarrassed and also didn't want to worry him about his care or my ability to give it. Plus, I wanted to run the unit, be aptly in charge, and get the promotion.

The problem I transitioned to was that the patient had HIV. He was a recovering addict and was very open about it, which at the time was quite rare given the stigma of the disease.

I ran to the bathroom to gather my thoughts and process my life. Composed and in denial, I slinked over to my station and began pouring peroxide onto my finger, squeezing it until it was blue. I futilely acted like it was a spider bite and I was draining the toxin.

Reluctantly, I finally confided in the charge nurse, Carolyn, who was intensely on protocol and precise—perfect for the role—not to mention a woman who dedicated her life to rescue dogs (so we got along well). She shook her head in a caring-yet-disappointed way and suggested that we report it and consider what was called PEP (post-exposure prophylaxis, or disease-prevention measures), which might include a hep B vaccine, hep B immunoglobulin, or antiretroviral drugs. There went my promotion.

I was immediately relieved of my shift, sent to the hospital emergency room to receive an HIV antibody test as a baseline, and would be tested again six months after my exposure. I was told to report any flu-like symptoms during that time—which, in retrospect, might have been the longest six months of my life. I kept imagining that I had flu-like systems and fought the feelings of embarrassment at work for having made such a critical mistake that we were all trained to prevent. It was like having my license revoked. I walked around socially feeling like a pariah riddled with a potentially trans-mittable disease. Only later did I humbly reflect on what life must have been like for that patient living with HIV and on dialysis, yet he was always so positive.

Data today shows that exposure to HIV blood has about a 0.3 percent, or one in three hundred needlesticks, chance of becoming detectable, and 99.7 percent of needlesticks do not lead to an infection.[4] The Needlestick Safety and Prevention Act of 2000 and OSHA's Bloodborne Pathogen Standards of 2001 have come a long way in helping to decrease nonsurgical needlestick injuries and make them easier to report. Still, many needlesticks go unreported.

As of this writing—twenty years later—I remain negative to all bloodborne pathogens, but I will never forget the experience or how I handled it. And today there are many new technologies, including devices with safety features and strict protocols, to help prevent needlesticks.

In a strange turn of events, years later my beloved Weimaraner, Hailey, overdosed on a bottle of Rimadyl. (It tastes very good to dogs). She was admitted to Cornell's veterinary ICU and needed dialysis to remove toxins and clean her blood, because her kidneys were failing. She was extremely stressed, not eating, and not thriving. Recognizing that humans share similar principles to canines, after a week I suggested we bring her home and let me dialyze her or offer at-home subcutaneous fluid treatment (peritoneal dialysis). "What?" my husband asked, adamant that my idea was a terrible one. But my vet and I have a very tight and trusting relationship so, a few days later, Hailey was at home in a warm bed with a blanket as I ripped open a drip set, inserted a wide-gauge needle between her shoulder blades, and let 1,000 cc of fluids flow. She went on to recover happy and healthy at home—the same as any human would

4   "Exposure to What Healthcare Personnel Need to Know," Centers for Disease Control and Prevention, Department of Health & Human Services, accessed December 9, 2018, https://www.cdc.gov/HAI/pdfs/bbp/Exp_to_Blood.pdf.

desire—thus proving that renal disease and dialysis continue to serve as the universal healthcare case study for me. As many who work in dialysis say, "It's in the blood."

THE JOB NO ONE WANTED

About a year into my job at the dialysis clinic, I took a lateral assignment on the reservation of the Tohono O'odham Nation. The reservation consisted of four separate land bases that encompassed a total of 2.8 million acres and a population of more than twenty-eight thousand people.[5] I wanted the job because I thought it would be rewarding, but also because I was being given even more responsibility. I knew that this assignment would carry a lot of weight if I did well, because the conditions weren't optimal.

Soon after I took the assignment, I found out one reason why it was so easy for me to get it at my age (midtwenties) and with my limited experience—no one else wanted it! The trip south was seventy-two miles down Arizona State Route 86, a two-hour drive one way, four days a week. It was a long, dark journey through the Sonoran Desert. It's part of the world renowned for its amazing, star-filled night skies. The road went along the base of Kitt Peak—about seven thousand feet above sea level at its summit—the site of a collection of research telescopes and programs for stargazing.

The clinic conditions were also less than ideal. It was certainly not the most modern facility, and I was on my own except for another patient-care tech who occasionally went with me.

My only real obstacle to the job was that, at the time, I still had the lemon Honda I had bought from the lot next to the Motel

5   "About Tohono O'odham Nation," http://www.tonation-nsn.gov/about-tohono-oodham-nation.

6 I had stayed at when I arrived in Tucson. It constantly died and then would only start with a jump or roll down a hill. I didn't know when I bought the car that it was a victim of Tucson's infamous flash floods—it had been submerged in water at one point in time. While it had managed to get me around town, it wouldn't do for that near-one-hundred-mile journey to the reservation. So, I went to the local Volkswagen dealership to see what kind of deal I could make. When I rolled in, the guys were laughing so hard I thought for sure I was going to end up with another lemon. But I negotiated and left with a tricked-out, cherry-red Volkswagen GTI that was superfast and had ice-cold air conditioning. I would later gift the GTI to my mom and it turned a horrific orange from the Florida salt and sun.

Traveling back to town at night had its moments. I've notoriously had a lead foot, but rarely got pulled over for speeding—probably due to the remoteness and special status of my job among the locals. One evening, while driving back to Tucson with a patient-care tech, Ryan, the headlights of the car illuminated something in the road. I squinted and could just barely make out four skinny, small, dark objects on the highway. They were legs—the legs of children just slowly walking across the road (or so I thought). I screamed to Ryan, "Kids in the road!" and he slammed on the brakes. The car skidded off into a large saguaro cactus, which, while terrifying, is significantly friendlier than a brick wall. I got out of the car and was about to head over to the road to make sure the kids were okay when I heard a very loud "moo." Turned out, those legs belonged to a gangly cow, standing there snorting at me, upset for the interruption to a nighttime stroll. I was so embarrassed to have mistaken the cow for kids, but so thankful that we hit a cactus instead of something far worse.

Interestingly, areas of the land where I worked expanded across the border into the Mexican state of Sonora. These same areas today are ground zero for the immigration debate that is making headlines as I write this book. The Tohono O'odham tribe has stated that, in their language, there is no word for "border wall." The nation has only the San Miguel Gate to access its land south of the border with the US, and its members and their animals that live there, in Mexico, are actually US citizens by blood. The Indian reservation is considered to be sacred ground and it is, therefore, beyond executive orders to have a wall separating the north and south, although immigration laws now prevent tribe members from crossing the border freely. During my time in Tucson, I saw many border crossers hiking great distances over roads and sometimes golf courses in 100-degree heat to make it to America. I saw an infant die of dehydration—but it was clear that the child's mother took the trip knowing that what was ahead was far safer than what she left behind. No matter how you feel about the debate, there is a public-health crisis involved, especially for children who can't speak for themselves.

In fact, the state of public health was one of the life-changing insights—a gift, really—that I gained while working on the reservation. In that role, I discovered that access to good preventive primary care was a real issue.

As time went on, I was able to help train locals to become patient-care techs. It felt great to know that young students there would grow up to get technical and even advanced degrees in healthcare. Today, Indian Health services supporting Native Americans have come a long way despite a chronically underfunded budget, which is at even higher risk lately given its interdependency with the Affordable Care Act (ACA) and its funding source being dismantled.

With that reservation job, I learned early on that, sometimes, getting to the next rung of the career ladder means saying "yes" to any opportunity—even those that no one else wants—especially if it's important to the company you work for. Although I took the job at the reservation without really understanding what I was getting into, it turned out to be a great career move and solidified my passion for population health.

MOVING TO THE BUSINESS SIDE

That reservation job opened the door to the business side of healthcare, because I advanced into managing a few clinics in the southwest area. By entering the business side of the industry, I began to realize that it would allow me to take care of populations, not just individuals. It's not that I didn't want to take care of patients; I actually love hands-on patient care. I just really wanted to make a bigger impact and found that I could maximize my reach in certain jobs by taking care of larger swaths of the population. I wanted to learn about public health, and the more I learned, the more facilities I could oversee, and the more patients that could be helped. Plus, I began making more money—and so did those clinics. So, it was a win all around.

Admittedly, since I was so young and inexperienced, I really wasn't all that great at managing people—I oversaw people who were easily ten or fifteen years older than me, and I had a lot to learn. At the time, people were trying to form unions, and I wasn't joining in the effort. Plus, I had to address poor attendance and underperformance, which included firing some employees. Sometimes, my hot little red car paid the price—I'd find it had been keyed. I was too young to really understand all the politics but just knew that, at times, I was not welcome in certain circles. So, it wasn't all fun.

Early on, I learned that just because *you* want to do something doesn't mean everyone *else* wants to. So, I was fortunate to learn at that point in my career how to lead from behind. I became a very democratic leader; I tried very hard to find and work with people's strengths. For instance, I'd always empower someone to be in charge on each shift. If there was a quality committee, I would choose someone other than me to lead it. Basically, I tried to share the leadership and lean into those who had more experience on topics, being deferent to their expertise.

I started becoming really good at networking as well. I became great friends with Cathy, the social worker, who carried a lot of weight, connection-wise. I also became close with the nurse practitioners and the two physicians who were the medical directors of the clinic, one of whom shared a birthday with me, and they placed a lot of trust in me. So, I wound up also managing out and up and down. In this role, I learned the concept of healthcare leadership currency being "content and connections," so I worked on both.

I've always been someone who likes to connect with a wide array of people, someone who genuinely likes to see people live their best lives and become their best selves. I've carried those traits all these years, and they've helped me become a much better leader—on and off the job. In those early days, I did things like form a softball team to try to get people together outside of work. I'd help organize a happy hour on both Tuesday and Thursday nights to ensure all members of the dialysis team could make it to one of the gatherings.

I parlayed my nursing degree (content and experience in that degree) into roles in the business side of healthcare—that's where the true power is because it scales. That can be seen when a nurse sits on any board of directors. When business decisions are being made, she or he never misses asking, "What about the patient?" Today, regardless of what happens to the ACA, the patient is everything as we try to find the elusive mix of cost, quality, and access. Nurses were trained to look at that from the very start.

Nurses and nurse scientists conduct research that informs evidence-based interventions to promote health, as I did in dialysis. Lucky for me, I noticed the importance of my education and role early on. It's no surprise that many nurses find themselves in senior business positions. One example is Marilyn Tavenner, former administrator of the Centers for Medicare & Medicaid Services, who today serves as president and CEO of America's Health Insurance Plans. In fact, if you peruse any list of the *most influential people in healthcare*, oftentimes you will find a few nurses. And today there are many organizations like the National *Nurses in Business* Association to support the transition or ascension of these future patient-centric CEOs and business leaders.

Furthermore, since nurses are the frontline providers of care for older adults—in settings ranging from preventive efforts in primary care and communities to hospital-based acute care to care in long-term and assisted-living facilities—their ongoing efforts to build a scientific evidence base and improve clinical care will continue to improve quality of life for the nation's aging population.[6] In fact, one out of every forty-five registered voters is a nurse, and powerful organizations like American Nurses Association have made part of their mission to educate their constituency on the power of their collective voice.[7]

After getting a taste of the business side of healthcare, I began to look at how I could continue to grow my career. I knew that I could only go so far with the dialysis company, and, although my asthma was a factor in why I originally pursued work in Tucson, it ironically

---

6   Patricia Grady, "Advancing the Health of Our Aging Population: A Lead Role for Nursing Science," *Nursing Outlook* 59, no. 4 (July–August 2011): 207–209, https://doi.org/10.1016/j.outlook.2011.05.017.

7   Matthew Fitting, "Nurses, Get Out the Vote!" *American Nurse Today* 13, no. 9 (September 2018): https://www.americannursetoday.com/nurses-vote.

is not a nirvana for asthma sufferers and the dust and swamp coolers often made things worse. In considering my next career move, I remembered how intrigued I was by the Amgen (Epogen) sales representative, so I began to research the top pharmaceutical firms in the industry. I decided to apply to the marketing department of what was then one of the best drug companies in the world—Merck & Co.

On paper, my brand was clinical—a nurse—and Merck often targeted businesspeople for marketing and sales roles, which required me to create a strategic pivot in my skill set and brand. So instead of focusing on the clinical experience, I highlighted my dialysis business building expertise and finance studies that I had completed, working toward a master's in business administration. I wanted to expand my personal positioning and develop my brand, and the skills I had acquired on the job and in the courses I was taking toward the MBA gave me the right to do that. My hook or pivot was to focus on a therapeutic area I knew well: asthma.

In the letter, I made the case for why a nurse asthmatic with leadership experience should be a candidate for the team that would be launching the company's asthma drug, Singulair.

Instead of approaching human resources, I put together my resume and a cover letter and FedExed everything directly to the company's head of marketing. I used green recycled paper for the documents so my paperwork would stand out in a sea of qualified candidates. And it worked; my hook and pivot was enough to get a face-to-face interview!

IN RETROSPECT ...

Looking back, I now see that the first rung of my career was about getting on the ladder and gaining solid footing.

The early years are the time to find your passion, get experience, and begin taking your path forward. Notice who is a mover and shaker—and not only in your own company but industry. Also, model your career journey on people you respect and admire, as I did with senior nurse leaders, doctors, and some of the drug and medical-device industry leaders who called on me. Almost anyone will talk about their career and journey with you if you ask them to share it.

Along the way, use the content acquired from training, on or off the job. During these years, you may have to take a risk, take the job no one wants, or make a lateral move to collect the content to go higher.

The first rung is also the best place to start your network, a list of connections that you will turn to for various insights and other purposes as you ascend. Back in the day, the Rolodex rotary business-card device was the "technology" used to keep contacts organized. I had more than one of those devices filled with contacts. I still call my contact list a Rolodex, even though today it's all digital and through professional social sites. Many of the social sites are like space with millions of constellations, so it's incumbent on you to work your network, as they do you no good far away and barely visible.

SECTION II
THE HEALTHCARE EXECUTIVE

CHAPTER 2
STEPPING UP

E mpowered with a background in the business side of healthcare from my time in running dialysis clinics and successfully
making the case as a business-savvy asthmatic, I earned the job
at Merck & Co. in new-product marketing.

I had made my case and nailed the interview in a hybrid clinical
role to be part of the launch team for Singulair. It would become
one of the most successful respiratory launches in pharmaceutical
history. (I say "one of the most," because I have friends who launched
Schering-Plough's Proventil and others who launched rival Glaxo-
SmithKline's Flovent, all of whom make the same claim. In pharma,
many have worked on "the greatest drug launch of all time.") I was
also responsible for opinion-leader and commercial-launch strategies as well as for policy and advocacy for the western region of the
US. I was basically what the world calls a "medical scientific liaison
(MSL)," which is the clinical talent used to advance the disease

dialogue around a new product launch. Many MSLs were nurses, pharmacists, and physicians. In today's new world of high-priced specialty medicines, a team like this should be focused on pricing, reimbursement, and policy considerations as they relate to individual patients navigating the system, especially those trying to procure a $100,000 medicine.

After another few years and a few stops in between, which led me back to New York, I was still looking for more pay and advancement, so I took a job at a multi-national company that was then called Sanofi-Synthélabo Pharmaceuticals in New York. There, I was senior marketing manager and led a joint-venture team of ten in the US and France. At that time, joint ventures between drug companies were quite common as a way of sharing in risk and reward. Then I moved into the role of the Heritage Brand business-team leader, where I oversaw roughly twenty products that accounted for more than $100 million annually. That was another job that no one wanted, because the drugs were dated, not sexy, and required zero marketing—or rather had zero marketing budget. But I learned the most I could from the financial training, and my team's efforts led to several millions in savings for the company in the first year. In that role, I learned financial forecasting and the head of the division was a sponsor who often brought me to the C-suite with him for financial readouts of my division. I spent more time with him than many of the high-profile launch leaders.

Then, in 2000, I landed a job with Pfizer, a pharmaceuticals maker that held a lion's share of billion-dollar brands and was, at the time, the place to work in healthcare.

It took a few attempts to get a foot in the door—I blew my first interview when I incorrectly recited the efficacy data for the drug I was interviewing to launch. A year later, when I got a callback, I was ready; I made sure I knew all the efficacy and safety data for every drug Pfizer made by memorizing a dozen product inserts, those tiny white origami papers included in the medicine's box. That landed me the job of marketing manager for one of the company's products, the anti-inflammatory Celebrex.

I've always been interested in strategy, in looking around corners to see what's ahead, so it wasn't long before Pfizer created a job and a promotion for me in which I managed the life cycle of its high-profile COX-2 inhibitor portfolio. Life-cycle management is the long-term planning for a product that runs through its patent life. Sometimes that plan exceeds fifteen years, depending on patent life.

While at Pfizer and commuting long hours on the train, I developed an academic interest and a career accelerant by studying strategy. The books *The Mind of the Strategist* and *The Art of War* were largely circulated around the Pfizer strategy teams, but that didn't satiate me. I found myself devouring books on power and military strategy. I was especially struck with military generals and their philosophies, e.g., Carl von Clausewitz, a Prussian soldier scholar whose teachings on war and combat have influenced many; my dog Claus is named after him. I could dedicate a chapter to his principles (and others), but the material takeaway for me was "make the best use of the few means at your disposal" and "simplicity in planning fosters execution." These principles have served me well in lean organizations and start-ups, which often have scarce capital. So, a good strategist recognizes that in a world of limited resources, your choices must focus on a material advantage that will enhance the chances of winning. And the best way I've found to do this is by telling a company, team, or your boss what they should *not* do. Be brave and rule out options. And as for simplicity, have a strategic slogan like I did with "10x16" (which you'll read about in chapter 3) and try to communicate in less than ten slides.

Working at Pfizer was an exciting and invigorating job, because the COX-2 franchise was so important to the company. In fact, that franchise was a major impetus for the acquisition of Pharmacia in 2003, creating a pharmaceutical giant with more than $48 billion in annual revenue, which has since been dwarfed by today's specialty biotech acquisitions. One used to buy an entire company with multiple drugs for $40 billion; today, some will pay $10 billion for a single drug. In fact, three of the largest takeovers in the industry's history were announced recently, with Bristol-Myers Squibb's $74 billion deal for Celgene, along with Takeda's $62 billion buyout of Shire and AbbVie's $63 billion acquisition of Allergan. These are deals I could have not imagined ten years ago, but today scale, earnings, and new science are the game.[8]

At that time, I looked around to see whose career I wanted to model mine after; who was my career role model? I didn't have to look far. Karen Katen was the president of Pfizer Human Health and responsible for the bulk of revenues. I had access to a high-profile consultant on my team named Lynn Gaudioso who was a consumer star, and she was an adviser to my life-cycle work, which included working on a "pocket pack" like Listerine for medicines. On numerous occasions, I also spent time with Maureen Regan, who not only worked on some of our product campaigns; she started one of the most successful healthcare advertising firms, which bore her name. My mom and I had dinner with her early in my career. She cared to know my family, which meant so much.

All of these high-profile women gave me time and inspiration, and they were fashion forward and fun in and outside of work, and

---

8   Ned Pagliarulo, "Big Pharma Deals Show Industry's Weak Spots," Biopharma Dive, accessed September 19, 2019, https://www.biopharmadive.com/news/big-pharma-deals-show-industrys-weak-spots/559659/.

Karen always gave me chocolate (Mr. Goodbars) along with honest and actionable feedback when needed. They all encouraged me to be myself and debate with facts and reminded me often that I deserved to have a seat at any board table.

One day, I was invited by a vendor to the Healthcare Business-women's Association (HBA) Woman of the Year (WOTY) event. The HBA WOTY is the healthcare and life-sciences industries' premier award, recognizing an individual who has served as a role model for excellence in leadership throughout her career.

I had been hesitant to join the group, because I commuted to Pfizer, which limited the amount of time I had for such activities, and because of my myopic focus on promotion and growth. Admittedly, deep down, I also didn't want to "rock the pink," a phrase I coined for what some men would infer when I chose to "spa" instead of "golf" at some early events in my sales career at Merck. I had hoped to make a list of top leaders someday, not just the list of women leaders often issued by rags. My views back then were shortsighted and dated. But I'm willing to publicly admit it now, since I knew others back then who felt the same way—something I think is worth noting.

Walking into the huge Manhattan ballroom where the HBA event was being held was awe inspiring and made me realize that I was missing out on an enormous network. The house was packed with women, men, and families of nominees, but mostly with aspiring leaders like me who wanted to be inspired.

As I meandered through crowds in search of my table, I read through some of the event literature, which included highlights of prior WOTY recipients. I was nearly stopped in my tracks by some of what I read. "Holy shit," I murmured while reading the materials. Not only were several of the prior winners my friends; they were the very people I was modeling in my career moves and actions. There was Lynn Gaudioso (winner 1996), Maureen Regan (winner 1997), and my very own Karen Katen (the first winner in 1990). Other future colleagues, friends, and board members would go on to win the award in years to come.

The experience validated two things: (1) I was good at picking and attracting winners surrounding my career and (2) the power of a female network is a career must, if not an enormous responsibility. I realized I had been getting a free ride and decided then and there that I was not only going to join the ride but take others with me.

Back at Pfizer, I spent a lot of time traveling up and down the elevator from the fourth floor, where I worked in one of Pfizer's first open-space concepts called the "fish bowl," to the C-suite some twenty floors up. In fact, before long, I earned the nickname of "staffer to the stars" from the Pfizer head of public relations, who was a wunderkind himself when it came to dealing with the press—and there was often bad press in the pharma industry.

The more the C-suite trusted me, the harder I worked, and the more sleep I began to miss. Every workday, I commuted to the Pfizer offices in New York City from my home in Fairfield, Connecticut, taking the train around five o'clock in the morning and then returning home after ten o'clock in the evening. To push through the grueling schedule, I sometimes power napped under my desk on a yoga mat with a fan blowing white noise to help me catch just a few minutes of much-needed sleep. I had two close friends who would wake me up if too much time passed, always chuckling at my "frustration-pencil hairdo" as I went about the rest of my day.

While being the "staffer to the stars" was a demeaning term to some people, I relished it for the access and visibility it provided. (In Washington, DC, and other high-profile locations, everyone knows it's the staffers that are responsible for getting shit done.) If you are good enough to staff a star, someday you will be the star. And maybe the people I worked with still see me as an invisible staffer or remember my career differently than I do, but it still doesn't matter, because it was an important part of the journey for me.

Besides, I was promoted almost every year I was at Pfizer, ultimately becoming the senior director of strategy directly supporting Karen and her office, which was in essence the main artery of Pfizer. In the strategy role, my team was on the hook for the company's strategic plan, the ten-year forecast for all of Pfizer's brands, along with just about any high-profile, pressing problem the company needed a team to help solve. I was also responsible for a huge swath of content for the quarterly earnings releases and the scripts for the analyst conference calls for Karen and many of the other executives.

The trust and exposure in that role were exhilarating. It was a huge responsibility for someone still in her early thirties. While in that role, other executives would also reach out for my review of their speeches and slides. They trusted my judgment and knew I had the content to do what they asked. No job was too small and I gladly slid speeches and decks under executive hotel room doors in the wee hours of the night with a sense of pride. But more importantly, they knew that, as an on-demand consigliere, I was brave enough to critique their message and tone, and that I considered the company's reputation as my own. As a result, I was often invited to the boardroom and was exposed to events above my pay grade.

But with the strategy lead role came an increasing amount of missed sleep, life, and fun. I used to wear concert T-shirts under my suits as a way of being hip and edgy, but in truth, they were just very comfortable for the long hours—sort of like corporate pajamas. I also splurged on a few pairs of Jimmy Choo heels for my wardrobe, which gave me some height and power. My choice of attire made me even more visible: at one point, an executive team member noted that I was wearing the same Rolling Stones T-shirt two days in a row and was stunned when I told him the reason—I had not gone home overnight. Although I dragged a green camping cot to work at one point, I never actually used it—the power naps were one thing, but to resign to actually "camping" overnight in my office was bit much.

There was a lot of extra pressure in strategy, because the data had to be exact. One way to help the team get the critical nature of exactness was with a phrase I developed during that time, and which I still use today: "Who is last man out?" This is often the last person on our team to leave work for the day, but it was also symbolic of the strongest and final link in our work products chain. This person had the final review of the stats, deck, earnings release, or formal team product at the end of the day. Often, that information was heading to the board of directors, a customer, Wall Street, or CNBC the next day to be used by analysts for reporting or forecasting. It was hard to pull it back once it was pushed off, which is why you coach many people to read an email twice before sending. If market shares were up 15.1 percent, that was the number—not 15.2, not 14.9. So, who was "last man or woman out" with that number? Often-times, when executives spoke, I was nearby, ready to give a hand signal if an answer was needed or wrong. The concept of "last man out" continued to serve me well as I ascended, and still plays a key role in my work. It's especially useful in dealmaking when it comes to term sheets, final investment decisions, nondisclosure agreements, and board decks. I remember getting a competitor's term sheet from a bank that reminded me of why precision in public-work products is mandatory for teams I lead. Clearly that team didn't have a "last man out."

I was at Pfizer during some of the company's greatest years and was intimately involved because of my life-cycle work when a major competitor (my former Merck) had to withdraw its leading drug, Vioxx, from the market. Given my life-cycle work on Celebrex, I was front and center with Pfizer's response and plan.

BEYOND THE WORKDAY

Like many executives, I was also juggling life outside of the workday. I really didn't have much time to exercise, and most of my social connections were quick drinks or clam chowder at the oyster bar in Grand Central, or "timing" a train with friends headed north to the suburbs.

During that time, I was also working toward a master's in public-health policy at Columbia University. Twice a week, I took the train uptown and then, after class, took the train back to midtown, where I'd catch the Metro North to Connecticut. On school days, I'd arrive home after midnight, then get up at 4:30 a.m. to catch the train back to work again. The only time I had for homework was during those hours commuting on the trains. And often my closest friend was Bauer, my Weimaraner, who kept the same hours.

Just like so many other executives, I also found myself dealing with a family-health scare. One busy day, I received a FedEx package at work from my mom, Nancy. In it, I was shocked to find her diagnosis paperwork: she had undergone an MRI that had revealed a brain tumor. I immediately called her and asked, "This is how you tell me you're dying—by a FedEx at work?"

She just replied, "Well, you work at Pfizer. Maybe you can find a doctor that knows this brain tumor."

As I've mentioned, healthcare is about content and connections. By this time, I was lucky to have both in spades.

With some reconnaissance and a distant connection, I found the top brain surgeon for my mom and her condition, Dr. Ed Oldfield, down at the National Institutes of Health (NIH). Getting my mom in to see him was no small feat, even with all my healthcare contacts—because a patient must "qualify for a study" to be seen at the NIH, since it's a center for clinical research. As Irish luck would have it, the cause of her brain tumor was rare and there was a team at the NIH studying it. Yet, even though he was the top man for the job, the first time he operated on my mom, he was unable to remove the tumor. I was more than frustrated; I was angry that the doctor I chose was so far away from her home in Florida, and still he had failed her. To me, it was like an Olympian balking a dive, like me tripping during a 400-meter track championship.

I told him, "Ed, you fucked up," which made everyone gasp, including all the dutiful fellows surrounding him, because no one called "the god of brain surgery" by his first name, much less spoke to him that way. There was no way I was giving him a second shot at my mom without a long discussion and a promise.

When I told my mom what had happened, she joked, "I knew it. You checked me into the National Institutes of Health. They operate on mice in this building, not humans." But Dr. Oldfield went back in and removed the tumor, which he reminded me was the size of the "O" in the *New York Times*. He clearly knew exactly what he was doing, balancing the risk of keeping her (and her open head) on the operating table too long and taking too much normal tissue versus going back in again and getting the tumor. He saved her life, and I thank him with all my heart for it. He has since passed away, but not before I got to thank him and personally praise him, which he knew was a big deal given all the work I did to get my mom treated by him. The NIH really attracts the best talent—a humble and heads-down cadre of science-minded clinicians—and I'm unsure it gets the public street cred it deserves.

Another plus: when I told my mom that he had originally missed the tumor, I had to tell her there was good news and bad news to lessen the blow. The good news was that, from then on, she and I would be taking a trip once a year to anywhere in the world she wanted to go. Then I hit her with "we need a redo on the brain surgery." She had a small dry-erase board to communicate with, since her face was split in half at the nose, and I'll never forget what she wrote clearly on that dry-erase board: "Shoot me."

Since then, we've traveled to nearly every continent, and if I even suggest that we take a year off or hit a local spot like New Jersey, she quickly grabs her head as if to pretend the brain tumor is coming back. I've spent countless bonuses on our trips around the world, and it's the best money spent. My friend Tom calls it "warm cash" versus the cold cash you bestow on heirs when you die.

What's interesting is that, throughout my mom's health scare, I sat by her bedside working on my laptop, because I didn't want to miss a beat at work. I didn't tell many people at Pfizer what was going on, because I was in a position that was not easy to get, much less keep. I simply could not be absent day after day—even if my mom did have a brain tumor. While I sat there, I wondered how many other people were out there struggling to hang onto a job while caring for someone they love? And what if children were involved? At Pfizer, a boss of mine with two small children lost her husband to a glioblastoma, and another went through multiple failed pregnancies. They couldn't call in sick—they just kept going and actually may have performed at their best when working through tough situations.

If you find yourself in such a situation, use your content and connections. Call someone who can help you get all the information you need about the disease and the top institutions that treat it. Those institutions are usually dictated by experience, research, and the physicians and scientists who dedicated their lives to that particular disease. Find out who publishes on the disease; that can help you see where the expertise is. After you have zeroed in on the center or hospital, use whatever personal equity or grit you can muster to get an appointment or second opinion. You may not ultimately go to that institution and may be guided by your insurance coverage, but the content will make you feel better about your family's medical plan.

A GSD MIND-SET

With all that was going on during those four years at Pfizer, I developed what I call a "Get Shit Done" (GSD) mind-set: wake up, show up, and put up the best performance you can, no matter how remedial the task.

> "Get Shit Done" (GSD) mind-set: wake up, show up, and put up the best performance you can, no matter how remedial the task.

Developing that mind-set happened out of necessity—it was the only way I was going to survive my ascent. I was already wired to the concept of medical triage, but as I began to apply GSD to my work, my focus became laser sharp. That's when I *really* began improving my performance and then rising through the ranks.

For instance, initially, I spent time trying to respond to every email. Then, a former boss told me how inefficient that practice was; he triaged emails by color-coding them and he rarely responded to emails he was copied on. I had also read the book *Taming the Paper Tiger at Work* by Barbara

Hemphill, which contained the system—file, act, or trash.[9] And there have been others like David Allen, whose system is closer to one I adopted, which I call ADD: act, delegate, or delete. Those three words really stuck in my mind, and from that point on, I viewed every task from that perspective.

> **Part of my GSD mind-set is triaging: Work on what's most important to the company, what's most important to the job, what's most important to shareholders. Triage meetings, triage the work product. Determine every week what needs to be done—and be maniacal about it. If it's not important to any goals, then why give it attention?**

If your company has a goal to grow by $100 million in revenue this year, ask yourself: What part of that should my division be focused on? What does "good" look like for the company, the division, the boss, and your role in relation to the larger company goals? And how is "good" measured? Don't assume the nonprofit hospital you work at doesn't have financial goals. Every work environment has a hard goal. Find it out fast, and make it your goal.

Once I gained that focus, anything that didn't point toward the goals began to peel away. Anything that didn't need to be acted on was delegated or deleted. I had one of the first Blackberries and would rapidly scroll like a slot machine, deleting and delegating like a champ.

Not surprisingly, my stress levels went down—I was no longer sitting up in bed in the middle of the night trying to catch up on

9   Barbara Hemphill, *Taming the Paper Tiger at Work* (Kiplinger Books, 1998).

emails or work. And if I did get up, there was a pad next to my bed that I could scribble on to get the idea out of my head.

GSD really kicks in on mundane tasks. That happened when I was on the hook for editing a big piece of Pfizer's earning script, which commonly had hundreds of version changes. Making those changes went well into the night and, in the era before iPads or personal devices, involved a lot of runs to Kinko's or back to an office or hotel room to make paper copies. To improve the efficiency of the process, I purchased a small, portable printer that was wheeled into the war room inside a rolling suitcase. I'd set it up and use it to print out revisions in real time rather than running around sliding decks under hotel room doors and then waiting for hours for the return edits from Kinko's. The executives' time was valuable, so in the spirit of act, delegate, or delete, I chose to *act* in real time. Years later, I bought a portable mini projector to flash slides on any wall in real time to accomplish the same task.

HAVING IT ALL—NOT SO MUCH

After four years at Pfizer, I chose to leave; this happened around the same time that Karen moved on. It was a sad time for me, because I was leaving one of my favorite companies, and because it had been so difficult to get in there, let alone ascend.

Trying to look around the corner at where the action was in the industry, I found a position with a biotech, Vion Pharmaceuticals, directing commercial operations and business development for a phase II and phase III oncology product. Unfortunately, though, the company had only one drug—and when it failed, so did the company.

I hadn't realized how binary biotech could be even though the data on the space was well published. Where big pharma companies like Pfizer had multiple drugs on the market, early days of biotech typically had a single specialized drug. In fact, it's estimated that more than 85 percent of new drugs fail to be approved.[10] We had placed a lot of debt on the company and, with a failed program, the company ultimately went into an organized bankruptcy. In the run-up to that, there was much debate at the time about laying off employees, because of the timing—it was right before the end-of-year holiday season. Was it better to wait until after the holiday so that people could celebrate unhindered? Or would it be better to let them go ahead of time so they could avoid spending money on holiday gifts that they might need to keep the lights on? In the end, the CEO aptly decided that waiting until January was worse because, like patients, employees have a right to real and direct information. It was an intense time, and at one point, a research scientist even told me, "You guys have no heart, Meg. No heart. It's Christmas." The executive team members felt terrible, but I learned a lot about managing when conditions are hard.

Up until a few years ago, I was so embarrassed by this experience that I wished it could just fall off my CV. (Do you have one of those on your resume?) But today, I've come to appreciate the failure—and even brag about it in the context of "fail fast and furiously." When you know you're going to fail, it's best to get on with it. That failure tested my mettle and put some tread on my professional tires, and I ultimately made some good friends at that job.

Following the experience at Vion, I decided to leave the demand side of healthcare and enter the access side, taking what some would call a less contemporary role with Medco Health Solutions. That job

10   Stephen D. Simpson, "A Biotech Sector Primer," *Investopedia*, Jan 24, 2018, accessed December 10, 2018, https://www.investopedia.com/articles/fundamental-analysis/11/primer-on-biotech-sector.asp.

required me to commute into New Jersey over the old Tappan Zee Bridge, which often turned into a parking lot. I had remembered Medco from my days working at Merck. At one point, Merck and Medco came together; a drug manufacturer and a pharmacy-benefit manager (PBM) vertically integrated. PBMs negotiate your drug benefits on behalf of an employer or payer. One can see why that might be problematic, and the two eventually separated. It seems ironic to me that today, healthcare plans and PBMs are vertically integrating—and the current environment is debating transparency around PBMs, with some even challenging their value. I've learned to be open minded about models in healthcare, since policy and competitive forces may present opportunities to revisit old models. It always bothers me when historians cite why healthcare models won't work because they failed before. Many models are often way ahead of their time.

Instead of being pigeonholed as a strategist—which actually isn't a bad hole—I asked for a dual job that would include a role in profit and loss. Being in a new role and having peak leverage, I saw that as an ideal opportunity to make such an ask. I was given that opportunity as the company planned for an expansion to Europe—an effort that was very important to the company. I spent the better part of a year with a team expanding out into Europe, including building de novo assets and joint ventures. Eventually, though, I was told that I needed to move there for the official president title and was even told, "Well, you aren't married and don't have kids like the other executives," and there was no other promotable position for me in the US except to stay in strategy.

I knew it was time to start looking elsewhere. I wanted to stay in the US because I had begun a relationship with Michael Darda, a prominent Wall Street macrostrategist, who would become my husband. During that time, I made the radar of a well-connected recruiter who vetted me for board and CEO roles, eventually highlighting a prominent post in Florida. That position wasn't right for me for a slew of reasons and, at one point, it really made me question what I was doing.

During my decline process, I was accidentally (or maybe not) copied on a string of emails *about* me. In one of the emails, the recruiter cruelly commented on my request to find a top job closer to New York because I was in a serious relationship. In a "mean girl" email, the recruiter referred to me as "a little girl passing over the big job for a guy." Instead of seeing my point of view as a woman trying to have a life, she viewed me as making a serious error in judgment and didn't hold back in her opinion.

That's just one reason why I've never believed in the idea of "having it all"—at some point, you have to make tradeoffs. I was nearly forty at the time, and my tradeoff was a choice that might be better for my long-term health and happiness. Hard choices like that seem to be common for women: they may pass up a job opportunity for love, or a child, or a family member.

At the time, the recruiter's comment made me feel terrible—I was worried that I might have blackballed myself, because she was very high profile and never called me back or offered me any more opportunities.

Still, I wasn't waiting around. I used my own connections to solidify two strong interviews: with Microsoft in Seattle, Washington, and Cardinal Health in Columbus, Ohio. I was leaning toward Microsoft and its emerging healthcare division, along with its formidable cash and market position. The company also had Health Vault, a way-before-its-time web-based personal health record created in 2007 to store and maintain health and fitness information. My trepidation with Microsoft was that, if I or the division didn't pan out, I was unsure whether the Xbox division would hire me.

Cardinal, on the other hand, had a nascent specialty division that desperately needed to GSD. The competitors McKesson and AmerisourceBergen had a combined market share of roughly 75 percent at the time, and Cardinal didn't even register. It was the ultimate build-and-come-from-behind story.

I was impressed with both of the leaders from these companies— technology pioneer Peter Neupert at Microsoft and George Barrett, CEO of Cardinal Health—so I was really torn about my decision with the opportunities they had available.

Reaching out for input from others, I met with a former leader in the very space I was pursuing. He helped build the formidable market share for one competitor but was now in private equity (PE) and was considered a titan of the industry. Sharing as honestly as he could, he told me I was nuts to take the Cardinal job. He said it would likely fail, since Cardinal was too far behind. I wrote his warning on a drink napkin while out in San Francisco—and would later tape it to my door at Cardinal.

Leaning toward Cardinal Health, I went on vacation with my extended family and friends at Lake Winnipesaukee in New Hampshire—another one of my dad's favorite places. As I sat there at the vacation house, drawing charts in my notebook while debating my life decisions, my mom came out on the deck with some news. By the look on her face, I could tell it wasn't good. She was pale and on the phone with the police: they had just found my thirty-four-year-old sister, Kiera. She had died in her bed of what we would later find out was an aneurysm. The police had been alerted because Kiera's shelter dogs had been barking for an entire day. The thought of my sister's dog, Annabelle, lying on her body as the detective found her is an image I'll never get over. (As I write these words, little orphan Annabelle is alive and well, living on in my sister's spirit.)

On hearing the news, methodically, my Mom and I took charge of the situation as if it were a business crisis. I summoned everyone out of the lake and up from shore to the house, where I told them what had happened. Next, I told them that my mother and I would be leaving for Florida to take care of my sister's affairs. I delegated notification calls to my competent and dear cousin Robin and tried desperately to locate the animal-control center that impounded Annabelle and my Mom's dog Barbara. I felt very much like the CEO of my household just leading, delegating, and executing a posthumous process. That's what my mom did at age forty-two when my dad died, and it's what many women do in and out of work, regardless of the problem they're facing. They lead quietly and GSD. That's why GSD has become my personal mantra.

The toughest part of that day was getting ahold of my brother Scott, who was working out at sea. We were so worried that he would hear of Kiera's death on Facebook. Eventually, his best friend, Kyle, reached him on a ship-to-shore radio. The news left Scott utterly lost at sea—another image I'll never forget. The news of my sister's passing was posted on Facebook, and since it was bad news, it of course went viral—it was very weird for a Facebook page to become an instant memorial and, of course, I couldn't contact anyone at Facebook to take it down or have any ability to alter it.

Mike and I knew at that moment that we would be part of each other's family, even if not formally. He has carried me and my family on his shoulders to this day. The people at the lake that day, including our friends, have bonded even closer because of how we came together as a team in what should have been a vacation. It's amazing how, in life and work, intense traumas or dramas bring out the best in people. And if they bring out the worst, it's okay to jettison that baggage.

Continuing in GSD mode, days and weeks later I vaguely remember contacting Peter at Microsoft and George at Cardinal to tell them what had happened, since it meant I would be delaying a start date. At this point I had decided to take the Cardinal Health job and was happy to be closer to home given the tragic turn of events. Both Peter and George told me to take as much time as I needed for what would be a major decision, or to pass for now. All involved showed real friendship and humanity as healthcare leaders and earned my friendship for life.

Back during my mom's illness, I remember what a physician friend told me while I was sitting on the steps of the New York Public Library and eating a hot dog during a lunch break while at Pfizer. "Meg, you have lost so much weight and I'm worried about you," he said. He gave me an order, as a doctor friend, "You must get through this—even if it means therapy, medicine, or a leave of absence."

Good friends will be honest and let you know how your coping is going, and you should look for their signal. You will get through to the other side no matter how much pain you feel at the time. And I used this same advice during my sister's passing, deciding to delay my start date for work.

CHAPTER 3

WHEN IT'S WORKING, THEN NOT

I n times of great stress and change, one of the greatest gifts of life is clarity. Sometimes, it's the only thing you can take away from tragedy or a setback.

After taking care of matters in Florida, my mom and I immediately returned to Lake Winnipesaukee to celebrate my sister's life, rather than mourn her death. But I knew I had to get back to work soon. After all, I was single and older, had a mortgage, and had one dependent—Bauer. In truth, work was a healthy endeavor that my soul needed.

Still, I was a mess with my sister's passing and pending job change. Just as had happened when I was dealing with my mom's illness, I was shedding weight and hair, and losing hours of sleep. But

I compensated by running ten miles a day to blow off steam. I felt like Forrest Gump—I only wanted to run. It was therapy for me, but my neighbor up the street, who saw me losing weight and running long distances at five o'clock in the morning, asked if I was training for an Ironman.

One of the most supportive people during that time was Mike, who would go on to help me complete three triathlons and the following year become my health-promoting husband.

In fact, everything was starting to normalize until one day, when I signed for a FedEx package that turned out to contain a letter from Medco challenging my noncompete in joining Cardinal Health. I took it deeply personal as the only thing I was expecting from the company was a sympathy card and a final paycheck. Mike calmly convinced me that it was an endorsement and, strangely, a compliment. "People don't want to compete against you, Meg, because you are top of your game," he said.

In the end, cool heads and a splash of legalese prevailed. Medco's fair legal challenge was a career nadir but a true gift of clarity. I had loved my time there; it was an important place to work at such an important time in healthcare. And the Medco network has turned out to be one of most powerful in healthcare. Many of my former colleagues and friends are now executives and CEOs around the industry.

In retrospect, the decision to join Cardinal Health or Microsoft was a high-class problem to have. Choosing to go with Cardinal Health included criteria of proximity to my home in Connecticut and flexibility, and Cardinal's assignment was paramount to the company. My criteria were largely personal given my painful and private transition, and while I would have liked to have kept the situation more private, the outreach of my friends in the industry was overwhelming. Many people gave money in my sister's name to orphan Annabelle and the shelter that she came from.

Two months later, I headed out for Ohio in a Mercedes after trading in the Saab I had inherited from my sister—a car that was on par with the flash-flood Tucson Honda. It was one of the few times I would drive from my home in Connecticut to my job in Ohio. I had bought a package of refundable airline tickets and thereafter "commuted" back and forth on weekends. For nearly seven years, I flew in and out of LaGuardia Airport in New York to Columbus, Ohio. Of all the jobs I had up to that point, Cardinal was my favorite—I made friends for life with many leaders there, one reason I kept going in spite of the commute.

The joke about Columbus is that it is one flight away from a direct flight anywhere, which means it often takes two flights to get there. Snowstorms were not infrequent, so if I missed a flight home on a Friday night, I just spent the weekend in Columbus because I had to be back to work on Monday.

HOW HEALTHY IS THE CORPORATE CLIMB? NOT VERY

When first starting a job, it's important to build equity in the company, especially with employees. When I joined Cardinal Health, I walked in as president of its specialty division, and I had never worked in the company. This was one of the reasons it was decided that I would not report to George Barrett, the chairman and CEO, directly as originally recruited. I would report to Mike Kaufmann, who at the time held the post of CEO of the pharmaceutical segment. At the time, this felt like a lateral or demotion but turned out to be a blessing in disguise, as Mike's team had some of the best operators in the business. And they knew how to make money—a rare but special skill. I had a front-row seat and instant peer group to learn from. This squad made the Cardinal trains run. In distribution, profits are so thin they are measured in basis points, so one must master operating and leading at scale. Once again, I picked winners, so a horizontal move wound up pushing me up a few extra rungs on the ladder but with more skills and confidence.

As a new leader, I made sure my first year was all Ohio—thus, the insane commute. That commute made it a little rough to get to the bosses' regular Monday-morning meeting. For me, it meant leaving New York on Sunday night. But that first year working at Cardinal, I made sure I was always at that meeting.

What I was doing was being a good corporate athlete.

Corporate athleticism has nothing to do with IQ or physical strength. It's about working on the most important projects at the company you work for, or for the CEO of that company—your goals should derive from one or both of those aims. It's also about figuring out how things get done, how a company makes money. I always say jokingly that "I know where the mob bosses are." I can figure out who is running the company, yet I spend time getting to know the company inside out, not top down. In fact, early on at Cardinal, I was taken aside privately by a senior leader to warn me about a "Thursday margarita night" run by some influential male VPs, which some felt were exclusionary—especially to females. I got the feeling management was trying to disband the group. The problem was I had been a brand-new card-carrying member of these margarita nights for a few weeks now. I had made it into this informal club and found it quite helpful to my own onboarding. Instead of ditching my new peer group, I feigned mock horror to this leader but stealthily went on to invite a more diverse set of peers, growing the complexion of the group.

Corporate athleticism can help you earn equity in the workplace. Once you have that equity, you can cash it in—like chips at a poker table. Build up a pile of chips, so that when you need them—it's snowing and you can't make it to the office, you need support on a deal, or you're going through a bad time in your life—then you've got enough equity in your role, in your brand, in your name, that you can cash in. I always want to ensure I have a pile of chips, because I never know when I'm going to need it. I may have a falling out with one of the "mob bosses," but because I built up equity, they may be willing to let one mistake slide.

Being a corporate athlete is an easier play under a great leader. Great leaders will set up a culture where you can take a measured swing and then fail without being put to pasture in your career. It's about being able to fail—ideally (as I've mentioned before) failing fast.

DETERMINED TO COMPLETE A DISSERTATION

On top of being a good corporate athlete at Cardinal, I was also determined to finish my dissertation toward a doctorate in public health (DrPh) at New York Medical College. Education and additional training are important to me, so I made them a priority, regardless of any sacrifice to sleep or sanity. That sometimes meant flying to New York midweek; I went to New York in the middle of the week like people go to dinner. Many people at work had no clue I was in a classroom in New York on a Tuesday night and then back in Ohio the next morning. That schedule was normal—until it started to go off the rails.

For my dissertation, my initial goal was to examine how effective insurance covering young adults up to age twenty-five (before really starting their careers) would be for the government and society. I felt that people at those ages, eighteen to twenty-five, needed primary care and coverage more than ever, especially with regard to mental health and smoking prevention. I thought it was a novel idea and worthy of a dissertation, but while I was working on it, the ACA was also being formulated. One of its major tenets was that young people up to age twenty-six could stay on their parents' insurance. There went my novel thesis.

So, I had to start over. I lost sleep and was really stressing over the issue, until I managed to channel all the negative energy into a topic that hit home—and ultimately became the reason for this book.

It happened on a rainy night in LaGuardia with a catastrophic delay that would inevitably have me missing work the next morning. That's when it hit me: I can't call in sick. What if I had a child at home—what do other executives, particularly women—in that situation do?

Ironically, I had met many women commuting to Ohio from New York weekly, some in fashion, some in politics, and some in business. Turns out there were a lot more women than imagined living parallel lives by catching planes, trains, and buses across the nation while working. To help put my three cousins through college, my Aunt Pattie has commuted by bus from New Jersey to New York for more than twenty years—a four-hour round trip.

As the information board flashed to "flight canceled," I contracted around my laptop for the evening like a nocturnal spider and started scribing in my moleskin notebook. That was a habit I had developed by then—carry moleskin journals color coded for various areas of my life—gray for work, orange for travel and life interests.

That's when it hit me: my new thesis would be about other people like me, women executives climbing and getting so close to the top of the ladder but waiting out a delayed flight in an airport lounge with yet another migraine threatening or a priority at home that must be triaged. As I sat there, I asked myself if there were other people, other women execs, who felt the same way? On that late night in the Delta lounge, I wondered how many women curled up in corners on phones and laptops were also failing at achieving the elusive healthy-work status. I immediately started scribing hypotheses to test and started to construct a study. The study of working women and their health became a personal mission. I wanted to prove that health status should be highlighted like pay parity or sponsors. It's a dialogue that should be happening in the workplace, and without it, companies may be losing out on talent and profits.

THE STUDY—(SOME) SURPRISING CONCLUSIONS

Given the lack of data on the topic, to answer the question, I would have to conduct my own primary research around executive women's health. Fielding a study added six months to my dissertation, as I had to find validated survey instruments and, that year, SurveyMonkey became my favorite tech company. It was ironic because, leading up to my paper, Sheryl Sandberg was getting a lot of the important press, but I was fangirling on her husband, David Goldberg, who was the CEO of SurveyMonkey.

The findings presented some surprising conclusions—and plenty of not-so-surprising ones—at least to women. Namely that the majority of women in the study reported good overall health—yet didn't actually *feel* that healthy.

My study found that there were plenty of people like me struggling with the psychosocial part of the climb to the top. To look at me—my weight is fine, I can run marathon distances, I appear to be fairly fit, but holistically, I had room to improve. For about five years during that climb to the top, I could only sleep at night if I took half of an Ambien—I called it a "halfbien." That's because I had made a living changing time zones and I was often stressed. So, there I was, a walking oxymoron: I was a senior leader in healthcare, and working on a doctorate in public health, but I really wasn't the healthiest person.

I decided to try to find out whether other women were thinking about opting out and why. There were data and stories of women opting out because of pay, sexual harassment, glass ceilings, or other reasons. But I was curious as to whether women wanting to leave the workforce or not making it to the top of the ladder as CEO had to do with their health. Did anyone just decide, "Screw it. I'm done with this. I'm tired of the commute. I'm sick a lot and want a better path." As several have said to me, "The juice is not worth the squeeze."

There had been a ton of great research on female-executive pay, but being a lifelong healthcare worker, I was curious if women at the highest levels of success eventually opted out to find more control of their lives and pay? Maybe their health was taking a long, slow, irre-coverable hit, which precipitated opting out early? I had several high-profile friends who left the halls of power to create their own halls.

While my thesis was around women executives, I also found that a lot of men felt the same way—there was almost a silent epidemic of stress for many senior executives climbing that ladder. I studied data on male workers on trading floors, firemen, and even night-shift nurses for inspiration into my study. These work environments were good analogs, given the evening and night hours and intensity of role while on shift.

The results were surprising to me since I assumed a large swath of senior executives would be unhealthy—physically and mentally.

According to my study results, that wasn't true.

But the results should not have been a surprise with regard to general health since executives typically have good private health insurance and good benefits. Yet, as it turned out, it was in the softer, more insidious types of health, such as mental and social health, where executives struggled. Most executives don't have flexibility and control over their time outside of work. According to a study reported in a 2018 issue of *Harvard Business Review*, outside of the nearly ten hours per day that leaders worked on average, they also conducted nearly four hours of business on nearly 80 percent of weekend days, and averaged more than two hours daily of work on 70 percent of their vacation days. Only about half of the average 62.5 hours that CEOs put in was actually at their offices. The other half was done at other company sites, during travel or while commuting, at home, or when meeting constituents.[11] Most of the CEOs I work with tend to speak or strategize with me on the weekend. It's the only unscheduled part of their lives. I don't know any CEOs who aren't available to give mindshare to their post seven days a week.

In my study, I found other factors such as the fact that executive women struggled with friendships. I found that to be true. Like me, some were quite close to the only friend that was available after hours—their pet. My dog Bauer (named after the famous brand of hockey skate because I'm a die-hard Rangers fan) was my best friend many winter months. He was up in the morning to see me off for the day, and he was there late at night when I got home. In my study, 19 percent of the women polled listed their pet as a best friend.

The results of my study made a lot of sense to women I knew— and to me—since women are master tacticians and deceptive over-

11   Michael E. Porter and Nitin Nohria, "How CEOs Manage Time," *Harvard Business Review* (July-August 2018), accessed March 31, 2019, https://hbr.org/2018/07/the-leaders-calendar.

achievers. I've had friends hide a pregnancy until month seven by wearing their husband's Brooks Brothers dress shirts over leggings, and several kept divorces on the down low. As I shared, I did not bring many of my personal problems to work, including my mother's brain tumor or my sister's death. I did not want to publicly dwell on that pain during office hours or have the problems overshadow my abilities in my new-and-difficult-to-obtain-and-hold roles. Those who did find out would genuinely ask, "Are you okay?" To which I took affront: "Of course I'm okay. Why? Is my work suffering?" Shame on me for not assuming good intentions, that a healthcare colleague would genuinely be concerned for my health as a patient.

In short, as women, we just GSD. Yet, it's not always with a focus on health, according to my study. And it's fair to say men may report the same, but my study focused only on women executives. In fact, a few journalists panned my study because men weren't a control group.

The following results highlight the need for a larger discussion about work and health in executive women:

- Forty-eight percent reported that they couldn't see a doctor due to workload.

- Nearly three in ten women reported using a sleep aid at least a few nights per week. The use of sleep medicines, coupled with troubled sleep patterns, left many executive women running a deficit. My friend Krissy used to call my landline at two o'clock on a Saturday afternoon and let it ring to wake me up. It was her way of saying, "Have a life. Goodbye." Single with no kids and work as my dominant force, Bauer and I became hibernating bears most weekends.

- More than 50 percent worked more than fifty hours a week and took work home, and one cohort worked enough extra hours to legitimately qualify as a second job. A typical workday for female executives often included nights, weekends, and holidays. Along with cell phones and iPads, work was a constant presence.

- Twenty-six percent used medicine for anxiety.

- Twenty-five percent wanted to lose more than twenty-five pounds, and 30 percent said that their change in weight was due to stress.

- The majority of women in my study felt that appearance played a significant role in their careers. Many of my friends have spent a small fortune on appearance and executive gear: bags, suits, and shoes for several seasons. I'm so grateful two young executives launched Rent the Runway so that many can enjoy feeling empowered without allotting a car payment to do so. And personally, I'm a big fan of the Fold and the RealReal, where you can get fashion-forward work couture for good value.

- Fifty percent exercised two or fewer days per week. However, there was a correlation with income with this stat—higher incomes were associated with lower BMI, even after controlling for age. It was thought that having more money gave a woman the resources to exercise; they likely had childcare, ate healthier, or even increased their interest in maintaining a healthier image. Many of my executive friends now own a Peloton that sits close by.

While the study didn't earn me coverage in the *New York Times*, it still informed on the social- and mental-health issues that affect females climbing the corporate ladder. My adviser and academic sponsor, Dr. Peter Arno, reminded me that data and primary research advance the field—and that is a worthy goal. To date, there has been very little on the study of executive women's health, although the few scholars taking it on have done great work. And in 2018, I was happy the topic scored an accolade through one of the best business books of the year: Jeffrey Pfeffer's *Dying for a Paycheck: How Modern Management Harms Employee Health and Company Performance—and What We Can Do about It*, which discusses how overwork, stress, lack of control, and insecurity impair employees' health—and even shorten their lives.

Lucky for me, a high-profile female editor at the *Harvard Business Review* could relate to my data around putting off one of her own medical appointments and helped my study get published online. Several scholars also contacted me for the questionnaire and study so that they could build on my work. That's all I wanted: a dialogue and public debate.

One point it did bring to light: most females are caregivers of others, even if they're not taking care of themselves, making work flexibility paramount. In my own experience, family illness and death both came at times when I was feeling intense pressure in my attempts to continue the ascent. As I mentioned earlier, I couldn't call in sick and, in the case of my mom's tumor, I might have been able to take time off to care for her, but at what cost to my career goals? I had to manage both, as many other women do or will do.

PEAKING IN HEALTHCARE

When I helped lead the relaunch of Cardinal Health's Specialty Division, which was struggling when I arrived, we implemented an audacious goal that was branded *10x16* —because we wanted to achieve *$10* billion in revenue by *2016*. That became our rallying cry, and we even had it printed on T-shirts. However, in the beginning, we missed our forecast for several quarters at a company that was known for making every quarter. It was tough sitting through board meetings during that time, especially with a peer group of operators who hit their plans. I knew that what we were working on was an important pillar to the company, and the strategy needed two years, but we needed to get results. I began to wonder if I was going to keep my job. Cardinal was an operating company, and we were building a new business, and sometimes—especially inside large companies— that can take time. It takes a company with patience to grow a division, and many just don't have that kind of patience or air cover with shareholders. Fortunately, Cardinal had some patience, allowing me to help lead a division that ultimately grew from $700 million to more than $8 billion in revenue on my team's watch—or around the time I was promoted to running strategy and mergers and acquisitions (M&A). That building experience will forever be a career headline—I was leading an incredible team and made some lifelong friends during that ascension together.

Remember this when choosing an assignment: try to understand if you are building, fixing, or accelerating a business.

Remember this when choosing an assignment: try to understand if you are building, fixing, or accelerating a business. They are very different horizons and skill sets. Those who accelerate may get more credit at the time than the person who inherited a turnaround or chose to work on a struggling product. Ultimately, in my experience, the more difficult assignments give you the street cred for earning a top post like becoming a CEO. Today, I'm in PE, and I put a premium on CEOs who have turned around a company or distressed product launch. A manager at Pfizer used to joke that anyone could sell and market Lipitor.

The specialty team at Cardinal went on to hit that 10x16 goal under a new leader that I recruited while I was promoted to running strategy for the company, and I was so proud. My hope with the new strategy role was that I would be in New York more often. But since I sat next to the CEO, it meant spending even *more* time in Columbus.

Eventually, it gave me a chance to take inventory. Sometimes you hit a point in your career where you have to ask, "Am I going to retire here?"

After seven years at Cardinal, I needed a change professionally and geographically. I had been in healthcare for over twenty years and had worked my way up from the emergency room to the boardroom. I loved building things and working with people, and I began to feel that maybe there was a way to share the lessons I had learned along the way to help build people in another capacity. And I had joined Cardinal when the stock was in the thirties and was leaving just after it kissed the nineties. It was an epic ride, and I was lucky to have picked a winning company and amazing stretch with fantastic people.

IN RETROSPECT ...

The healthcare-executive period of my life was a continuum of my belief in content and connections. I succeeded, in part, because I learned to be overprepared, a discipline that would go on to serve me well in senior roles. And I loved staying close to movers and shakers.

I also discovered and began to develop my GSD brand—once I learned to act, delete, or delegate, my work product and results really kicked in. GSD became my personal brand—I became maniacal about it and it really blossomed at Pfizer when I was a staffer. I learned to triage the top priorities and make short-term or spot goals in order to reach long-term goals. Short-term goals let you see what's planned for the week ahead and give you measurable steps toward achieving something greater. Since they are manageable building blocks to success, they are ideal for keeping you healthy in work and in life. Spot goals are also a good discipline to have: What is the goal of this meeting? What does "good" look like this month for me? Spot goals can help you zero in on immediate wants or needs, and they help you achieve your short-term goals. I read once about a US president who had ten-minute meetings, and often folks would get a double slot, if needed. I love that idea. In fact, I think corporate America would do well to adopt it. Why fill an hour if you don't have to?

Every day is a chance to make things happen. No matter what gets put in front of me, I triage and then treat it like it's an important assignment and do my best work around it.

It was also a time to learn how to manage through

tragedy, something that is highly personal and more likely to increase in frequency as you go through life. You will have unforeseen events that gut you. That's important to know early in your career, because tragedy will find a way to triage itself to the top of the list, whether you like it or not. How you respond is dependent on who is around to support you and your own coping mechanisms. During times of great strife (job change, being fired, divorce, death, or deep financial trouble) I have found that one must focus on survival. You must work hard to put this one moment of many in your life into perspective. As my dad shared days before he died, "Meg, this is one of many bridges you will cross." At the time, it felt like the George Washington Bridge had fallen on my head. One of the most important lessons I learned happened while I was at Cardinal after publishing my study—I learned that health is your wealth. Granted, it was relatively late to learn such a valuable lesson, but I have also worked hard to make up for lost time. I have become an academic on the topic by studying it closely and am now in a position to share the lessons and potential traps for those I teach.

Probe deeply on whether your job affects your general health, sleep, exercise, medication use, and psychosocial elements of your life. If the boss is toxic, don't take the job, and if you are just realizing how unhealthy your job is while reading this book, start looking for an exit ramp.

THE ACADEMIC

CHAPTER 4

KEEP LEARNING

When I left Cardinal Health, I did not have another position to go to, yet surprisingly, it was the most untroubled feeling I'd had in a long time. I was in my midforties— prime earning years—but was walking away from an amazing job at a company I loved, and, in the process, I was leaving behind all the pressure and expectations of the climb to the top. I didn't know if I would ever land the role of CEO at that point, but I would no longer have an insane

> I literally became an official member of my study—I was creating a better path for me, not opting out but opting up.

commute between New York and Ohio. I was heading back to be closer to Mike, friends, and my dogs—there were two of them now.

Yet, I was still driven, and ultimately that would lead to a very well-paying, prestigious job much closer to home. I literally became an official member of my study—I was creating a better path for me, not opting out but opting up.

One of the things that kept me busy during the first year after I left healthcare was the teaching role that I had already started at Columbia University. That role was a direct result of my pursuit of advanced education during the hectic years of climbing the corporate ladder.

That pursuit started when I enrolled in an MBA program and took as many night classes as I could fit in while working in Tucson at the dialysis clinic. And I even took the LSAT and pondered law school. In spite of that long commute for a job not many raised their hand for, I was determined to improve myself by taking classes in accounting and business finance. Since I was so young at the time—still in my twenties—and I was starting to take over management of clinics, I wanted to learn some business and leadership theory to bridge my wide gap of inexperience. I had a lot to learn with regard to managing leaders, some who were twice my age. I've since seen a lot of parallels to young tech CEO/founders who find themselves in a similar position. To them and others I say: never lose the gift of self-awareness with regard to your deficits. Many will ask you to talk about your "superpower," but few will help you acknowledge and manage your developing powers, including any possible kryptonite in your skill set or personality that can weaken your ascent.

While I've always believed that education is the ticket to growth, I've really seen just how valuable it is for opening doors. When I was getting my bachelor's degree, some of my friends in college had a famous poster with photos of yachts, Porsche race cars, and mansions under the headline, "Justification for Higher Education." But my justification was to have content, be prepared, and earn a seat at the table—those are important aspirations to have during the climb.

Eventually, I did get a slick black Porsche, but then nearly lost my license due to multiple speeding tickets on the Merritt Parkway en route to the medical school for classes.

Another reason for continuing with my education is that healthcare is in a perpetual state of change, especially with our understanding of the human genome, advancement of artificial intelligence (AI), the ushering in (and out) of the ACA, and all the vertical mergers in the last few years; in this industry, experience is like bread—it can stale quickly. Trends are always changing, and most of what happens in business is policy driven. Medicare and Medicaid largely pick up half the tab for healthcare in this country, and Medicare alone provides federal health insurance for more than sixty million Americans over the age of sixty-five, so with an aging population, if you are doing business in healthcare you are doing business with Medicare.

After I graduated with my DrPH, I met with a sponsor and friend, Michael S. Sparer, JD, PhD, who is a professor and the chair of the Department of Health Policy and Management at the Columbia University Mailman School of Public Health. Over lunch, he flat out asked: "What are you going to do with your doctorate? Teach, right?"

Teach? Me? Since I had never considered it, I had no idea what I would teach. I wasn't really an expert or a scholar on one of the important topics typically taught at that level—members of the faculty at Columbia are the best in their domains.

When I shared those thoughts, Michael asked, "What are you passionate about? What do you think is missing from our program?"

I thought about it and realized that getting my master's in public health at Columbia was an important part of my ascension in healthcare. Since healthcare is so technical in nature, getting a specialized degree with an emphasis on policy was crucial to my climb—or to anyone who is serious about that career path. I began to scribe a syllabus of what was needed in healthcare education: a specialized graduate degree tailored to both the capital side and the increasingly relevant public policy side of healthcare. Since healthcare is 18 percent of the gross domestic product of the US, I realized that getting ahead meant understanding "the business of healthcare." And there it was: the subject of my class.

As I write this book, I've been teaching the Business of Healthcare for five years and the subject is in demand, as I have a waiting list of students wanting to get into the class. In fact, the class has been so popular that it has attracted some of the nation's top healthcare leaders as speakers, a who's who of CEOs, policy makers, healthcare-technology innovators, journalists, bankers, and private-equity leaders. Michael has been so supportive that we were even able to arrange a filming of a pilot show of the class using an Emmy award–winning production team. The show, titled *Healthcare in the Round*, was filmed at the nearby New Balance Track and Field Hall of Fame, and was modeled after the format used in the *Inside the Actors Studio* television show on the Bravo channel (although our show never attained that level of popularity). Since I ran track for most of my life, being at the New Balance Track and Field Hall of Fame was extra special. I hope the topic becomes a podcast or someone advances the idea further than we did.

The class aspires to be at the intersection of public health and capitalism—two words that, together, are largely considered to be contradictory. But not for me. I think some of the greatest developments and solutions in healthcare have come from a mix of both private and public partnerships.

OPTING FOR EDUCATION

As an academic and business leader, I'm often asked about the value of getting an MBA versus a master's in public health, and when is a doctorate the next step? Higher education should come down to career goals and skill set, timing, and the school you get accepted into. Let me explain.

Goals and career. When considering your career goals, think about where you aspire to go and what is missing in your skill set. For me, healthcare was the short- and long-term goal. Since healthcare policy and regulation are constantly evolving, fresh content gives an edge—and I knew that education was one way of getting that content.

If you want to work in finance (a hedge fund, bank, etc.) then you should likely pursue an MBA or a straight-up master's in finance. And let's be honest, you'll never regret getting an MBA, as the network and skills learned will pay off forever. For me, advanced degrees in healthcare trumped straight finance and business degrees as I ascended. And even though I never aspired to do research or teach at the doctoral level, I wanted to perform at the scholar level. I envisioned being an executive academic. When I attended the WEF in Davos, Switzerland, or the annual meeting of the American Society of Clinical Oncology, I was a card-carrying academic and entered different dialogues and groups.

I was always curious about patient populations, policy creation, segmenting markets, and forecasting future population trends—all skills that were honed during rounds of advanced biostats, epidemiology, and the primary research conducted during my dissertation. In PE, where I am today, much of my time is spent on business valuation. I have found that the intense process and procedures learned in epidemiology forecasting and policy creation have aided in the mandatory discipline required for difficult due diligence analyses conducted before acquiring a business.

Timing and the school you get accepted into matter.

I've recommended nearly ten people to Harvard Business School for their MBAs, and many went on to graduate as Baker Scholars (students with highest distinction). I knew the phenotype and, as expected, most of them are crushing it in finance or consulting, and a few are running successful companies. All of them took two years off to attend the program and were very serious, honest, hardworking students. They all made the right decision given their goals.

When you consider your goals, also think about your reentry strategy.

It's very common for consultants and bankers to work a few years, apply to and attend a top-tier school, and then come back postgrad. In fact, it's typically expected. But that is often not the case in mainstream corporate America. If you take two years off, it may require a careful reintroduction analogous to taking an overseas assignment. In some cases, you must plan your return before leaving. Make sure your corporation and management are on board with your degree or extra training so you get credit versus being penalized for taking time away from work.

I was in the corporate flow of promotions at Pfizer and didn't want to halt that progression. Plus, I had no one holding me back. But are you considering a family, or do you have young children? Do you despise the cold but can only get into a Midwest program? Even if you didn't get into your first choice, or you have other commitments, or you want to remain employed but you think you can swing it, it's okay to consider a part-time or executive program.

There will be small regrets and missed opportunities as you ascend and evolve. Ironically, from my perspective in PE, I wish that there had been time for a master's in finance, but I'm doing my best to cover those bases outside of work. I have an entire section of my personal library dedicated to valuation, company building, and debt finance. And I live full time with a macroeconomist and strategist who models the market daily. He has helped me model and analyze the cost of Medicare patients, will test my assumptions or critique my math, or help me run a regression on any set of variables I muse about.

DO THE MATH

No matter what degree you pursue, you can never take enough math and finance. When students ask me about electives, I always tell them to take more math, finance, and strategy and increase their analytical prowess—these subjects are the foundation of everything and great equalizers, especially for female leaders who aspire to be CEO. It's really tough to get to the top without understanding profit and loss. Researchers found that 86 percent of payer and provider CEOs had prior profit-and-loss experience, but men are three times more likely to take on profit-and-loss positions.[12]

Regardless of position and level, take the time (especially in a new job) to understand how your company makes money. That will arm you on how the executives measure and approve investment decisions. Even today, in PE, some of my first diligence questions

---

12   Oliver Wyman, "Women in Healthcare Leadership 2019," *Women's In-House Counsel Leadership (WiHCL) Journal*, accessed February 19, 2019, https://www.oliverwyman.com/content/dam/oliver-wyman/v2/publications/2019/January/WiHC/Women%20In%20Healthcare%20Leadership%20Report%202019.pdf.

when looking to acquire a company are: How does your firm make money? Who pays you? Take me through the payment and reimbursement flows. Today I understand how hospitals, pharma companies, PBMs, distributors, and tech companies all make money in healthcare—and it's not only different; it's often intertwined.

Related to this as you ascend is learning to present a convincing business case for investing in a new project, medical equipment for your department, or innovation such as developing a new drug. The case is often based on understanding the return on that investment, or its ROI, which I cover in my class via example. Why would anyone invest in your project or idea if it doesn't have an attractive return? It's a frequent but terrible management pitfall to say, "But this deal is strategic." Some important financial metrics that shed light on an investment are ROI, net present value (NPV, which is the present dollar value of the projected future cash flows), and internal rate of return (IRR, which puts the return in percentage terms on the dollars invested to drive its NPV.) These calculations tell your boss, board, or investor how much profit the investment expenditure will earn over its life and whether it meets the hurdle for capital invested in your company.

Even if you never get an MBA, you should be familiar with your company's cost of capital, especially since it will be your job as senior leader and C-suite operator to approve the use of capital. If the IRR on a project or an investment is greater than the minimum required rate of return (often your company's cost of capital), then the project or investment is often pursued.[13] To make this easy, spend time with your company's CFO or a senior leader in finance. Take such persons to lunch and pick their brains on these questions.

---

13   Will Kenton, "IRR Rule," *Investopedia*, February 17, 2019, accessed February 19, 2019, https://www. investopedia.com/terms/i/internal-rate-of-return-rule.asp.

And get specific; ask them about the last few deals or investments and how they are performing.

At Pfizer, I spent a lot of time calculating NPVs on drug-development programs, comparing them to each other in order to determine how to prioritize among them. While many of my peers were working on cool direct to consumer campaigns and high-profile launches, I was spending my time on what-if scenarios and modeling for Pfizer, a skill and peer group that would forever serve me well. The NPV calculation was powerful in telling the company which programs it should *not* pursue.

In corporate M&A and now in PE, I spend a lot of time presenting IRRs and MOICs (multiple of invested capital, which measures the value an investment has generated) for my projects, driving decisions around which ones to pursue and at what price. And today, in PE, many firms seek to exit an investment (sell the company) within five years and shoot to generate an MOIC of two to four times and a 20 percent IRR. In deal circles, if you return five times back what was invested it's considered a home run. As a business leader you should consider several valuation metrics, as the investment period and speed of growth for the investment matters. With asset prices at historically high levels, leaders must have an angle on an upside or synergy to justify paying premium prices as they think about future exits and returns. The basic concept of ROI has followed me since my time in dialysis and is a basic metric in healthcare regardless of whether you save lives in an emergency room or lead a company in the boardroom.

THE "BUSINESS OF HEALTHCARE"

Because I believe so strongly in education as a foundation for one's career, I wanted to make the class I teach at Columbia as real world as possible, as if the students were on the executive team of a Fortune 500 healthcare company. I wanted to give my students the ability to apply real operating experiences learned in my classes to their current or future jobs.

When putting together the class, I knew I was up against some heavy hitters. I was adding a new elective in a school filled with high-profile electives—like Chelsea Clinton's class on global health (a class I'd love to take). Also, Columbia is at the forefront of public health and policy—armed with the best faculty in healthcare. So, I knew I had to work hard to make sure that my class was fun, interesting, and relevant. In fact, I always tell my students that I want to ensure they're getting their money's worth, and they laugh and tell me, "You're the first teacher that has talked about their class like it's an investment." Back to returns, education *is* an investment in your career and should have an ROI.

Basically, I'm teaching what has been the last few decades of my life and in a format that the students really enjoy. Part of the class involves hands-on learning through visits to area healthcare interests, because I want students to have unfettered access to these companies. For example, we sometimes conduct a "live lab" at places like the CVS MinuteClinic, which, to the people working there, is like the TV show *Undercover Boss*. The president of CVS MinuteClinic has hosted our lab three years running. In another class session, we conduct a "mock CNBC television hit"—they simulate the role of a CEO/CFO sharing their earnings or recent merger where they have to defend the strategy and use of capital in less than two minutes. It forces one to get to the point and control the narrative. Or we might spend the class time at a high-profile start-up. In one class, we visited Flatiron Health, a healthcare technology and services company that is conducting cancer research. There, we met with Flatiron's CEO, Nat Turner, and the students interacted with other members of the management team, people working in an open setting accelerating cancer research or programming code. Shortly after our visit, Flatiron was acquired by Roche for $2 billion. The students were so inspired that a company focused on making care better for cancer patients could trade for such a high price. And I always give my students real questions or investment decisions I'm currently evaluating, from "What should Rite Aid do next?" to "How does Amazon win in healthcare?" I'm dealing with really smart healthcare thinkers and leaders; why would I ask them bullshit questions when they can share important views on questions keeping me up at night? And I always ask for predictions. It's amazing how prescient some of the leaders in my classes have been. Recently, we were discussing the importance of being good at managing government lives, especially with regard to Medicaid and Medicare. And we highlighted Centene as one who does Medicaid particularly well and was musing on its next move. The next day Centene announced plans to acquire the company WellCare in a $17.3 billion deal. This new company would have combined revenues of $97 billion, serving twenty-two million individuals across all fifty states, including twelve million Medicaid recipients and five million Medicare recipients.

THE BUSINESS OF HEALTHCARE: "REFORM AND CONTEMPORARY ISSUES FOR PUBLIC HEALTHCARE COMPANIES"

COURSE DESCRIPTION

The aim of this course is to provide students with an overview of the major public healthcare companies that influence and shape the US healthcare system and the current policy challenges faced by these entities in light of healthcare reform. We will focus on "purchaser, payor, provider, and policy maker" targeted within the Fortune 500. We will cover companies including pharmaceutical, clinical care, medical device, managed care, technology, and emerging business models. We will discuss pressing issues such as value-based healthcare, transparency, technology innovation, consumerism, reimbursement pressures, and the new role of government that affect all players. We will highlight the intersection of public players with the new era of healthcare reform that is forcing innovation and change in a volatile marketplace. Attention will be given to the drivers of cost, efficiency and quality in relation to pricing, innovation, and the evolution of how healthcare is financed.

DEFINE YOUR FUTURE

Throughout my life, I've refused to be pigeonholed. That opened the door for me to attend an Ivy League school, Columbia University, and go on to earn a doctorate. I went from being a middle-of-the-pack student in high school to being someone who once made the Wikipedia page for Fairfield University as a high-profile nursing alumnus. Don't let high school be the end all be all—it's a tough place to find your future self in four short years and everyone has the chance to reinvent their own brand. And I did this with honesty and hard work, as there was no easy path for me or my siblings—just hard work over a long, gradual climb.

Too often, I see people hold back because of their situation, earlier life experiences, or their own self-limiting mind-set. I lost my dad as I turned eighteen, and thereafter, it sucked to be in high school and worrying about my mom and money for school and life. Getting a waitressing job at night, passing class, and ensuring I had a track scholarship became my sole priority—not getting an A in AP English.

When I worked on the reservation, I saw that pigeonholing in effect in a direr form. In fact, an article in the *New York Times* reported on the negative outcomes for Native American students, in part because of their circumstances. The article reported that Native American youth have the highest rate of suicide among people ages eighteen to twenty-four: twenty-three per one hundred thousand. (By contrast, suicide rates in white youth are fifteen per one hundred thousand.)[14]

It's never too late to reinvent yourself. With education, experience—and pluck—you can get the *big* job and reset your path. The best part of my job on the reservation was watching young students with huge promise ascend into healthcare jobs as dialysis patient-care techs taking care of their own. And many of my students at

14   Erica L. Green and Annie Waldman, "'I Feel Invisible': Native Students Languish in Public Schools," *New York Times*, December 28, 2018, accessed January 2, 2019, https://www.nytimes.com/2018/12/28/us/native-american-education.html.

Columbia have gone on to become such things as a *New York Times* star journalist, influential policy leaders, CEOs, entrepreneurs, and hardworking doctors and nurse leaders.

Sometimes, getting ahead also means simply asking for recognition. There were times when solid "asks" for help were what I needed to meet my professional goals. One of those came after I had been teaching at Columbia for a few years with strong student reviews. I had started out as an adjunct and guest lecturer while I was still working at Cardinal. But I was so intent on the students getting value, and I was working so hard to make that happen, that I was spending basically the equivalent of more than two classes of time doing prep work. So finally, I asked for formal recognition. I didn't expect to get tenure, or even monetary gain, but I felt it was time to ask.

I was granted the title of adjunct assistant professor, and then adjunct associate professor (which I didn't ask for), both titles that validated the work that I was doing. I treated my teaching job like all my promotions in corporate America—I asked when appropriately timed, and when the recognition was given, I was grateful. It's important to note that I had the goods and track record to be in a position to ask. And the ask was reasonable; I wasn't trying to take a tenured track spot that I didn't deserve or just get a parking spot with my name on it in front of the medical school.

NEVER BE ABOVE LEARNING

I was once called a "surprisingly poor presenter" after winging a presentation at Pfizer. There was no way I was going to go through life with that label, so I went downstairs and joined the company's Toastmasters club the following day. There were a lot of raised eyebrows;

people wanted to know why a senior strategist and one of Pfizer's "fast trackers" needed training in public speaking—shouldn't I already have those skills? But I told them I needed to know more—I needed new tools so that I could be better than I was.

I've never been above learning in any form, not just through a university. Whether it's continuing on with your education, taking additional training, spending a month reading strategy books, or signing up for a single class or seminar, find the time to supplement your knowledge to help you make the best of your craft. Today, there is so much content online, from TED Talks to top schools posting their classes and lectures for free. And you can transition into healthcare or make a career change with a two-year degree or certificate or a postbachelor's track in nursing.

Personally, I'm impressed with the online format, especially Khan Academy, which is spectacular for math tutorials. Check out its statistics courses—you won't be sorry. In 2017, while on Martha's Vineyard, I had an idea around advancing associate-level trade degrees in healthcare like nursing, pharmacy tech, and respiratory therapy, for example. I drafted a business plan for an online program for graduating high school students, which included an extended "lab" internship modeled after my class. Students would work via a mix of online and real-life labs. I envisioned that, after graduation, they would receive offers in the very institutions they trained in as students.

> **Whether it's continuing on with your education, taking additional training, spending a month reading strategy books, or signing up for a single class or seminar, find the time to supplement your knowledge to help you make the best of your craft.**

After months of online theory, the program would then include a live lab at a top institution (center of excellence) and those entering healthcare would be off to a solid start on a strong base with a top education and a job. Those with these special trade degrees could enter the workforce immediately, start earning a good wage, and then go back for more education or a four-year degree and there would be an opportunity for reimbursement by the institution. I recently read about a janitor at New York University's Tisch Hospital who, after cleaning rooms and watching patient care, went back to school and became a nurse at the same institution.

I got a soft intro (spot sponsor) and spoke to Salman Khan, the founder of Khan Academy, about the idea and maybe working with me in my classroom. The goal was to use his best-in-class platform for future healthcare technicians in nursing pharmacy, respiratory therapy, or even a new degree like "chronic-care technicians," using his site as the hub, then partnering with various top-tier healthcare institutions around the US (Cleveland Clinic, Tenet) to offer the live lab-training piece of the degree. What is so amazing about Khan Academy is that it is focused on getting people in the workforce via education and ultimately to get a paying job.

My idea didn't progress mostly due to inertia, but I'd gladly turn it back on if someone called me. And I still think a "chronic care" trade degree is an interesting business and academic idea.

It's totally understandable if you can't afford to continue your education on to a master's level or beyond, or you don't have time to go to school because of family or other commitments. But if that's your situation, then look into other ways of learning. Identify areas of improvement, and look for ways to improve your knowledge or skills in those areas. If you're weak at finance, there are plenty of online training classes to take, or find a work mentor. I've been a "strategy and M&A mentor" for so many leaders who simply asked. If you're terrified to speak in public, Toastmasters is free to join. It'll often put a group on your campus if you can get more than five or ten people together. Maybe put together your own training—do others need to learn something as much as you do? Do you have access to someone who is great at a skill that you don't have? Not being able to afford an advanced degree is no excuse to stop learning or honing your skills. There are many ways to make yourself better at your craft.

And remember to look for those opportunities when you're ascending: when I took my first jobs in the industry, tuition reimbursement was a mandatory criterion for me (Merck had that benefit).

A wonderful training opportunity that Cardinal offered while I was there was called StrengthsFinder, which is used by many progressive organizations. Instead of finding a person's weaknesses, it focused on top strengths. It also identified the strength of a team, which helped its members understand each other's strengths. Through StrengthsFinder, I confirmed that I'm more of a strategic thinker and influencer—I'm stronger in ideation, analytics, and vision. So, now I know that if I am involved in a project with a lot of details, I need to delegate those detail pieces to someone else on the team. Understanding that at Cardinal allowed me to spread the work around based on where people's strengths were, so they would have low risk to lean into it and also low risk to get the assignment done.

Sometimes when I'm working with people, I'll ask them how they're doing by asking them to share their life and work in a pie chart or apply some math to their time commitments. This quick analysis and dialogue lets me know when they are in the wrong assignment or job. For instance, if someone tells me he or she has been working on a modeling forecast for four days alone in a cubicle, and I know that the person is an extrovert who aspires to sell, then I know it's the wrong role—and he or she is certainly not in a state of flow. That's something everyone who has worked for me knows: I'm always asking, "Are you in flow?"

"Flow" is state of performance discovered by psychologist Mihaly Csikszentmihalyi. Flow is when you are working at optimum performance levels, because what you're doing doesn't really feel like a job. You're giving 100 percent to a company, and in return, it's giving you even more enjoyment back, because you're working on something that you really like. You forget it's work. You look up from your work and, holy cow, it's three o'clock in the afternoon, and you can't believe how much you've gotten done. That's flow.

Now, sometimes work requires you to do things that you don't want to do, and maybe don't really excel at. You can't always be in perfect flow. But if you're not in flow the majority of your time, then you're probably in the wrong job. A boss once reminded me when I complained about using our new HR performance software, "Some parts of your job suck; this is one of them."

BE A LEADER OF HIGH CONTENT

I pride myself on being a leader of high content—and that's been one of the keys to my success. Having high content—in other words, being very informed about your industry, your role, your team, your project—can help you when in a conversation or in front of a room.

Having content requires that you overprepare for the expected and unexpected moments. Rehearse presentations out loud. Take notes to organize your thoughts before speaking. Have an angle or sound bite. I was once told to write down my thoughts before speaking, which would not only prevent me from overtalking but would also allow me to have a potent point. Read industry rags; in fact, read everything you can about your industry, including what's going on with competitors. It's your job to be a good participant, invest in the prework, and earn the money being paid for your time. The first thing I do upon waking is read in bed for thirty minutes about my industry. I ask myself, What is happening in my field? My Twitter, email, and alerts are rigged to give me this download first thing in the morning. It's also an easy way to ease into your day with a cup of coffee, to get your mind going before taking on more important tasks.

Another way to prepare—and overprepare—is through journaling. As I mentioned in chapter 3, I developed a habit of journaling using different-colored notebooks for various areas of my life. I make work a craft and use visuals to help me learn and communicate ideas. I have used work journals since 1997 and still have all of them. Most of them are about my performance or ideas; I draw a lot of charts to socialize my thoughts and ideas before sharing them in prime time and have them turned into slides by team members. I have a lot of energy and like to ideate, so my journals serve as a way to help me organize my personal work product. I also have sketched over twenty business-plan outlines in these notebooks. Whenever there is a major shift in the market or a new policy, I often scribe what business model is now needed. One note on journaling in a litigious world: no one wants to think you are the lawyer scribing the team's thoughts and words. One board chair recently said to me, "All that writing is making me nervous." So, make sure the journaling is discreet and appropriate. And I once had a former boss leave his journal in a conference room. The journal's contents were unfortunately circulated around the team and were found to include personal comments about direct reports, including one who had bad breath.

I still journal to this day. On Sunday evenings, I look at my week at a glance and make sure I can deliver on everything that's scheduled. Do I need prep time for any of my meetings? Did I ask for a deck or preread? Do I need to move a meeting around? These days, I sometimes ask whether I need a particular meeting. Then, I wake up every day and imagine, "What does 'good' look like for today?" If I have seven meetings in one day, it's likely not all of them are equal.

But I've seen leaders apply the same concept in other formats than journaling. I've seen them walking down the hall putting note cards in a pocket or scribbling on an iPad. No matter the format, noting your ideas, your day, your future can help you be better prepared—and can help you triage.

Having a brand will also help you when it comes to content. Everything you write, do, and deliver is a product of *you* and an extension of your personal brand or positioning. It's just like with any other product: a Volvo, for instance, is considered safe. As another example, I have a friend who always says she is like a pair of Vans sneakers: "edgy, cool, and ready to hit the jump." What is your positioning, your personal brand?

My brand is my "Get Shit Done," or a GSD persona, and that started very early, before it was even titled. Part of that includes something my mom instilled in me back in kindergarten when she told me, "Always do your best work." And if you ask me to do something, consider it done. Take it to the bank. I aspire to have my work product always be first rate. On the first night of class, I ask my students to develop a short bio; it forces them to think about their positioning. You can also do this on Twitter—how do you describe yourself in 150 characters?

As a young child, a teacher encouraged me to have a special work space to be creative and it was a desk in the basement where I could create or break things. If you can, have a work space in your home or apartment that makes you feel energized. In grade school,

I frequently won design contests: one was for a book cover (I built a rocket showing that reading will take you to the moon—how appropriate) and another was a hat contest that featured my favorite stuffed animal—Kermit the Frog leaping out of a top hat with confetti.

Similarly, in business, a senior woman mentor once told me, "Leave a job or assignment better than when you arrived." That is a form of best work. Make sure your fingerprints are there and noted. Be known for delivering top-shelf work and that brand will follow you wherever you go.

IN RETROSPECT ...

Education and knowledge were instrumental to my ascent no matter how grueling my schedule was. Earlier, I described the crazy-busy years at Pfizer. Back then, getting my master's degree meant taking the A train uptown to 168th Street and then back down to Grand Central to catch the only Metro North out of New York City to Fairfield, Connecticut, where I would arrive home around one o'clock in the morning. And during the years I was pursuing my doctorate while at Cardinal Health, it occasionally meant flying back to New York midweek from Columbus, and then turning right around and showing up to work the next day.

As you ascend, it's important to be conscious of the impact you have on other people. I believe all leaders have a responsibility to inspire those around them, and it's not just altruistic. Positivity and followership will encourage teams to do *with* you and *for* you.

Finally, take math classes at any time during your career. I hope you see the ROI in that.

SECTION IV
THE DEALMAKER

CHAPTER 5

REACHING THE PEAK

The first year after I left healthcare, in addition to working as a professor at Columbia and consulting, I actually took some time off. I mapped out a bucket list year of activities that were personal, professional, and vocational. I had the backstop of sitting on boards and teaching. Those two roles kept me in play—even though my career was less dominant, my brand was still active. I was on Twitter, attending conferences, writing articles, engaging new leaders, and leveraging my now fortress network quarterly.

During that time, I took a nonprofit trip to the Dominican Republic with Trek Medics and its founder and my friend Jason Friesen, whose slogan is "Bringing 911 where there is none." We spent the time training the local population to become emergency responders and outfitting them with motorbikes and sidecars, which served as off-road ambulances. The genius of Trek Medics, among other things, is that the organization recognizes that healthcare around the world is largely local, and, during crises, populations trust and respond well to their own.

I also jumped out of a plane over Dubai with my mom for her seventieth birthday, took a family trip to India to see the elusive tigers in Ranthambore National Park, and went to the Coachella music fest with my girl squad to see Guns N' Roses reunite.

But there were some pitfalls that year as well: I laid to rest my beloved Weimaraner, Bauer, and supported my younger brother Scott through a cancer diagnosis and battle.

I also spent that year investigating a future in PE, maybe one of the most difficult career pursuits to date. I was now a forty-six-year-old woman, which would have been the prime age to be a CEO. But I was pursuing a role in PE, something more commonly reserved for men that had already been a CEO or leader of a corporation. It was a significant change that concerned quite a few of my acquaintances—they were worried that, if I took myself out of the running for a CEO position in healthcare, I might get stale. I didn't close the door on being a CEO, but instead of waiting for offers, I was exploring my options.

Despite over a trillion in dry powder (slang for cash) and new funds emerging monthly, managing money in PE is one of the most elusive clubs in the world for both males and females, but especially the latter, with only 10 percent of senior positions in the industry being held by women.[15] The week I wrote this chapter, there were several articles in the news about how twenty-two-year-olds in the industry were getting $300,000 starting salaries because talent is the special sauce in the industry. That kind of pay breeds shark-level competition. (I was lifeguarding at that age.)

---

15   "Women in Private Equity," *Prequin*, March 2016, accessed November 6, 2018, http://docs.preqin.com/press/Women-in-PE-2016.pdf.

According to respondents in the annual "Women in Alternative Investments Report," there is some progress toward employing more women in the PE industry, but most believe that it's still harder for them to obtain capital or to succeed.

In spite of these stats, given my depth and success in healthcare and all my dealmaking experience, I thought the odds of a role in healthcare PE were in my favor. It seemed like the ultimate hurdle to overcome, and I loved the idea of how competitive the field was, so I wanted to see if I could figure out what it was about and whether I could win a job in the field.

What I learned is that retired senior execs, like ex-CEOs, can become a "senior adviser" or "operating partner," roles that don't always invest directly but, instead, they advise, consult, and help the portfolio companies operate and achieve their investment cases. I wasn't senior or experienced enough to be a legitimate titan of the industry ("We need some gray hair in this meeting," one person said to me at the famed J.P. Morgan Healthcare Conference), but I was well past being an entry-level leader, post-MBA, or investment-banking job hire. I was a square peg, stuck in a middle hole—a place I'd worked too hard to rise above—so I was certain I would not stay there long. A lot of people tried to push me toward board work only, but I was determined to get a job.

During my year off, I dabbled by setting up my own consulting shop, GreyGhost Advisors, named after my Weimaraners, and a few friends in PE also allowed me some free exposure to their field. One, a successful friend and senior leader in the industry at TowerBrook, allowed me to join the firm's annual meeting where investments are presented to the limited partners, or investors. There, I could "try out" and find potential matches that might need my expertise.

Unfortunately, I didn't make a match, but I got to see up close and personal what matters to PE and how leaders in the industry think about investment horizons, debt, management teams, and returns. I was enamored with the idea of business building and making things better with patient capital, strategy, and teams, although I didn't care for some of the short-term horizon views. I also learned there are different firms and approaches, and that family offices or long-term funds would likely fit my personality.

Although I thought I was a natural fit, my unique role as a Fortune 50 operator and strategist didn't translate. Still, I was grateful for the free exposure and used it to meet other firms around the industry, only to find that my pocket was often picked. Everyone was open to taking my ideas for free with the promised opportunity to "join our board *if* we get a deal done." Ultimately, it was my fault for not figuring out the right narrative or demanding fair pay for my time. A few tenured friends laughed when I told them about working for free, hoping to land a permanent spot later. But I was prepared for the opportunity should it knock again or in the way I wanted. Today, when I use expertise or consultants, I always pay them regardless of whether a deal gets done.

Undaunted by my early experiences, I circled back to thinking that maybe joining a PE portfolio company board would be a fair start and give me exposure. That became a reasonable short-term goal that I put out to my network, and then waited for something to strike. In the meantime, I got right back to my year of adventure and paid consulting.

Then, one hot summer day, a senior friend of mine asked me to serve as his reference when he was recruited to be a CEO of a PE-backed oncology service. Over time, I have come to dread giving references, because writing them takes a lot of work to do well; they require honesty to keep your brand intact, and oftentimes, people ghost you until they need a reference—big mistake. And I was a little green with envy—my friend had received a PE CEO call without even trying out for free. Since I believe in the responsibility to advance the next generation of leaders, and a good reference can open doors for all parties involved, I put the reference together—his was actually easy to do because he is just that good. As luck would have it, he had offered my name to several PE shops as a potential hire.

Before long, between surfing waves, I found myself dancing on hot sand in the shade in Martha's Vineyard on what I thought would be a ten-minute call with a team from a PE firm. An hour later, they asked me if I was interested in working in PE. "As an adviser, operator, or full partner?" I probed. After spending a year learning about it, I knew that I only wanted to be a partner. I didn't want to be an operating partner or an adviser or just a board member. I wanted to manage money, and I knew that my strong traits in strategy and organizational development were valued in company building, which some PE firms pursued. I just needed to match to the right firm.

Turns out the job was a full partner for a long-term fund with close to $25 billion under management, but that, more importantly, had a desire to put $3 billion into healthcare that year. The job as described was perfect based on what I had learned up to that point, so I began to conduct some deep diligence on the firm, team, and position.

I really loved the team because they were all the people that I could not be, and they were wildly smart, which is always attractive. They were prior investment bankers, had worked their way up to PE, had lots of experience, and were willing to onboard me to PE. What I brought to the team was decades of healthcare experience, including some technical skills in M&A that could be transferred over to PE. Once again, I was parlaying prior experience into the experience I wanted. They wanted someone with my experience to hunt in an area that I knew really well—biopharma services. So, it was a perfect fit, and I joined.

Then I called allies to help cover PE topics that were foreign to me, like debt financing. I called David Gluckman, vice chairman of investment banking and global head of healthcare at Lazard, and over lunch we discussed my challenges, aside from brainstorming new deals. He set up for me a "Debt 101" class (which was more like 102) with the top debt guys at Lazard. Being a professor, it was fun being the student, and the Lazard team allowed me to ask novice questions in a safe setting. Again, it's an important lesson to never be above learning and to use your contacts to help you improve.

But I had no clue how to construct my employment contract, fund documents, or the carry structure, which is how PE pays *if* your deals go well. Many deals don't go well or hit their investment cases, despite what is reported about the industry in the media. I called a few acquaintances in PE and was dismayed to find that, in this business, many quickly turn into competitors. The first questions I typically encountered were, "How much do you have under management?" and "What are you focused on buying?" I also found out early on that people would use me to price a deal and then walk away. I had a lot to learn. But I did have two strong managing-director friends who were intellectually generous and, to this day, still call me to work on deals together (syndicate), which is the ultimate compliment in PE. A friend who is a PE recruiter gave me guidance on salary, bonus, and carry numbers. Back in corporate America top executive salaries were often buried online, and with some digging you could get your range and negotiate. And yes, you should always negotiate but never blindly, as you can be way off in either direction. Salary is like high-stakes poker where it's legal to count cards and triangulate your position through data and questions while never revealing your hand until the end. At a minimum, and if totally lost, simply ask, "What is the range for this position?" so you have a data point.

In the first few months of working in PE, I vented the challenges to my husband and a former boss. They both chuckled and told me, "It's finance. A lot of money changes hands, so the stakes are high. Don't let it change you." I was reminded by many friends and colleagues that my unparalleled Rolodex and strategic abilities around business building would enable me to make a small dent in this industry. Well, it didn't feel that way. I felt outgunned and underprepared at every turn.

I had used my best asset to finish my diligence on the role. In performing that due diligence, a few people gave me some harsh feedback: I would be working for wealthy international businessmen at a time when it could be politically problematic to be associated with foreign nationals, especially Russia, they said. But I also called two friends at Allen & Company and asked to talk with George Tenet, who was a managing director there but more importantly the former director of the Central Intelligence Agency. That call and other contacts put me in touch with several station chiefs and global experts in US intelligence. Having a history of immediate family members in the FBI, I knew what questions to ask.

As for that onerous contract, one early morning I found myself on a Washington-bound flight sitting next to famed attorney Bob Barnett, who has represented countless presidents. I carefully befriended him and felt inspired to send him an email asking if his team—particularly one very strong female lawyer, Deneen Howell—could represent me on all the areas of my agreement. They did and it helped me immensely.

Postdiligence and contract, I felt 100 percent confident that the business leaders I was joining in PE were not going to appear on a "no-fly list." In fact, my employer turned out to be a Ukrainian-born, United Kingdom and Israeli card–carrying citizen and entrepreneur who worked hard for his success, had a burning desire to build and own world-class businesses, and who cared deeply about the next generation of leaders, including me. Since then, my employers and our expanded team of global business leaders have shown me nothing short of high ethics and an impressive understanding of healthcare and business building. They also have shown me the sobering realization that nationality can be a perceptive disadvantage, although not insurmountable, in building world-class businesses. If you have a patient approach to capital deployment and are good, you can win.

In my three years as a managing partner at L1 Health LLC, I have worked on three deals. One was a multibillion-dollar healthcare-services deal, one of the largest private healthcare deals that year, and the other two were truly "buy and build" strategies which was my initial thesis for where my skills might be valuable in PE. One business was a de novo start-up we called K2 Healthcare Ventures focused on investing in new biopharma companies, and just recently we closed on an animal health services deal acquiring Destination Pet and committing to putting $450mm into the space. The work is extremely interesting, and I feel lucky to have landed in a senior role that fits my skills and personality. With these investments, I helped to select and recruit management teams because of my Rolodex, and I help with the business-building strategies. My background in the healthcare industry and GSD have served me well in this role.

For our first portfolio company, I invited a former competitor to be our chief commercial officer. While I was at Cardinal Health, the pharmaceutical powerhouse AmerisourceBergen dominated specialty services and was the reason I was told during vetting of Cardinal to pass on the opportunity. The specialty services division's leader was a real badass, and every day I had to deal with her team's successes. To my team's testament, we worked very hard to chase that division in those years.

Now long out of the industry, I met her eye to eye in a dark, dank midtown bar in New York City to recruit her to join me and our team. We both laughed because the meeting was a long time coming. She joined and, as expected, is killing it in PE. Plus, she's adding a noticeable dent to the list of female C-suite executives. And, of course, we became good friends—another powerful connection, locked and loaded.

"THE LIST"

One day, after I had been happily in PE for two years, the phone rang. A top executive recruiter called about a search for a senior leader to "lead health for Google," and my name was on "the list." Or this great woman simply put me on the list. The call came out of the blue—I had not been pursuing a CEO or any other leadership role in healthcare since I opted into PE.

Still, it was Google. So, when I came home, I told my husband about the call and he had a lot of questions: "Wouldn't that mean going back into corporate—and in California? Didn't you just move to New York and work your ass off to get a PE post?" In truth, without any direct technology experience, I didn't really think I would be a top choice. While I've always loved technology and have been an early adopter of everything that can digitize and scale my life, the bulk of my healthcare career was before AI. I did, however, have an edge when it came to healthcare data; my career was built on it, and

I have always had a great affinity and aptitude for it. I felt I could make the bridge.

Since the Google job was, at the time, possibly one of the best jobs in healthcare, I thought I should click on that search and see what was on the other side. Even if I didn't want or get the job, the interview process itself—meeting with Google execs and learning more about AI and other nonhealthcare companies focusing on healthcare—would build my knowledge base in PE and maybe even bring me some new connections. I decided to interview.

Over a weekend, I sequestered myself on Martha's Vineyard and went through a cord of wood going deep on AI and all the data Google published on the topic. To my surprise, Google spent a lot of time and money on healthcare despite not taking a formal vertical in the space.

After doing all that research and preparation, I ended up making it through the first round of interviews and went to dinner with Jeff Dean, who ran AI for Google—he is basically the rock star of the coding world. The tech mag *Wired* even called Jeff "so smart he doesn't need AI."[16] Being around him gave me a front-row seat into how powerful AI could be in healthcare, and he was quite humble to discuss it. I was convinced that the plague of unstructured healthcare data, which is its own bureaucratic epidemic, could be well served by AI. It could help those on the front line and payors reduce variation and launch a broader set of analytics to ensure we have the right view of patients and their clinical and financial needs. The sheer brute force of deep learning could help patients get the right care at the right time, since, for many, like my mom, Google is their entry point into health—really their first visit.

---

16 Tom Simonite, "Google's New AI Head Is So Smart He Doesn't Need AI," *Wired* (April 18, 2018), accessed February 20, 2019, https://www.wired.com/story/googles-new-ai-head-is-so-smart-he-doesnt-need-ai/.

For me, intellectually, I saw a larger opportunity to materially address the more mundane problems around eliminating administrative waste and inefficiency in our system. Right now, most of the need in healthcare is boring and not very sexy, as a senior friend at a Fortune 50 pointed out. He has thousands of employees doing healthcare work, but 25 percent of his workforce is in administration, which is crazy. He asked me how AI could decrease this number to 10 percent—so that he'd have more people doing patient care. I had made several acquisitions of companies in the machine-learning space, but nothing comes close to what I learned about Google's team and capabilities. And one of AI's advantages is about the data collected, which only means we are in early innings of what AI can do in healthcare globally.

So, while the CEO dream call had finally come, I was unsure the timing was right for me given how much fun I was having in PE. In the end, Google chose a rock star, David Feinberg, a doctor that had run Geisinger Health—someone I would gladly work for. Instead of being disappointed, I was elated to have made the list as a contender, and the door was left wide open for me to potentially work with the company in some other capacity. So, the process was good overall—I met some incredible people, I learned a lot about AI, and there might still be some opportunity there. In the meantime, the experience is making me a better healthcare investor. I've also learned that a lot of companies have an advanced Excel product and not AI.

Sometimes it's okay just to be on "the list," even if you don't get the job,

Sometimes it's okay just to be on "the list," even if you don't get the job, as you have to play to score.

as you have to play to score. The Google interview was yet more proof that success is a product of three things: education, experience, and a powerful network.

Interestingly, when recruiters today ask me about roles for which they are seeking senior leaders, they often follow up with: "If not you, then who would you support for this CEO post?"

When I review my own list of bulletproof CEO candidates, I find that it consists of roughly two women for every eight male candidates. This is a major issue that needs to be addressed. A cadre of powerful leaders have placed me on their list over the years, so now that I have the power, I do the same for other women.

While women in healthcare make up 63 percent of entry-level workers and 58 percent of managers, they represent just 31 percent of senior vice presidents and 25 percent of C-suite leaders.[17] It also takes women longer to become healthcare CEOs. On average, it takes women three to five years longer than men to reach CEO, depending on the organization.[18]

In my efforts to help develop and champion more qualified female candidates, I crafted an email with the subject line "#TheList" and sent to it my professional contacts. In the email, I requested that they name at least one qualified female candidate for a high-level position. Immediately, about half the group wrote back with a name. By the end of the day, my email had been forwarded back to me twice from women I didn't even know. And *Fortune* ran a nice piece on the mandate: "A C-Suite Job Opened Up. Do You Have Any Women to Recommend?"

Fortunately, my email also generated positive feedback from the influential men I sent it to. In fact, one male CEO from a Fortune 100 company gave me his initial recommendation, and then later in

---

17   LeanIn.Org and McKinsey & Company, "Women in the Workplace 2018," accessed February 20, 2019, https://womenintheworkplace.com/.

18   Oliver Wyman, "Women in Healthcare Leadership 2019," *Women's In-House Counsel Leadership (WiHCL) Journal*, accessed February 19, 2019, https://www.oliverwyman.com/content/dam/oliver-wyman/v2/publications/2019/January/WiHC/Women%20In%20Healthcare%20Leadership%20Report%202019.pdf.

the day, came back with a second name. While the idea of having "a list" clearly resonated with him, it also solidified why having those names at the ready can be so powerful.

For the idea of a list to be successful, however, women need to understand the importance of helping other women. That takes diligence and, in all honesty, humility. Earlier, I mentioned the AmerisourceBergen division badass that I recruited for a C-suite position. She was without question the best person for the position. But having competed against her daily in a previous role, I had to first check my own ego before I put her in play.

I'm not advocating having lists of leaders that include women simply to fill spots and help company statistics. There is nothing worse than taking a risk on filling a top slot with a woman, and then seeing her fail publicly—we all lose from that. Worse, I've witnessed companies putting women into lower profile—even safe—roles so they fail safe and news can be buried and not require a financial disclosure or press release.

Inclusion on a leader's list is about *earning* the spot, regardless of gender. It's about ascending as a life sport and, with that mind-set, reaching the top of your game.

Inclusion on a leader's list is about *earning* the spot, regardless of gender. It's about ascending as a life sport and, with that mind-set, reaching the top of your game.

What I am advocating is that leaders have a personal pipeline of other leaders that they develop and trust, a list that they can readily provide to businesses looking for high-level candidates. That list should include women and diverse candidates, because endorsing broad experience sets for high-level positions benefits all of us. As another CEO coach reminded me, "Don't pass trash and be surgical in your endorsements." I worked in one company where a senior male leader was passed around divisions, despite having terrible performance reviews year after year. It was a bad a game of old maid to see who would pick him next.

MORE FREEDOM TO CHOOSE

When I think about what I wanted in my twenties, it was financial freedom—the ability to own a nest and car and to take trips. In my thirties, I wanted a life partner, more travel, and as much education as I could fit in my brain. I wanted to climb and grow like my favorite plant, the saguaro cactus, and I knew that education was my ticket to life's success—like a ride up the elevator in the movie *Charlie and the Chocolate Factory.* That rocket to the top, like the book cover I drew in first grade, would mean that I had made it, and I was determined that education was the golden ticket to that winning ride. I knew all along that education had the amazing ability to set you apart and give you big wings of courage. It is a great equalizer if you can access it.

At the same time, I was conditioned to live below my means, probably derived from when my dad died. After that happened, I knew to only buy what I could afford and not run up a bunch of credit card debt—which is not only fiscally irresponsible but often leads to additional stress I didn't need. Even today, when I tell people I grew up in Connecticut, they always immediately assume Greenwich, a town I love by the way. I'm mildly amused to respond, "No, Norwalk." Norwalk is a diversely hip, artsy town. We focus on places that are safe, quiet, and dog friendly and allow easy commutes to work and teaching. My husband is obsessed with minimizing (starting before there were books and TV shows) and using all of our space, saying, "All 1,700 square feet of this house is used," and there is no waste. It's always about living below our means and not being unhealthy or wasteful about it.

In short, I've had to learn the important lesson: it's not about winning; it's about getting what you want with your health intact. I remember wanting to make $100,000, to prove I wasn't average. To me, that was not only symbolic of success; it also seemed very far away from what I was making as an entry-level nurse. But if I was honest with myself, that initial $100,000 was really only about bragging rights, or winning. It didn't really address what I wanted.

You see, in spite of how it may appear, I never really wanted to have it all, and never assumed that was a good goal. I just wanted to get out of the middle, and keep moving forward and up. Like a great medicine, I wanted to keep adding on with my own line extensions—education, wealth, prestige, contribution, and life experiences. It was a big deal to me to be able to change an industry, build a division, help someone get promoted, get a friend to join a board. Those are really the kinds of things that spell success to me today. Every time I get someone on a board, help a graduate, or see a friend promoted, I brag loudly and publicly.

Today, I also know what I don't want on the climb to the top. And when I reached forty, even greater than my aspiration to be a CEO was my desire to help mint other CEOs. That was more rewarding. I have put a premium on things I don't want, like migraines, drama, or money stress, if they can be avoided. And I've found that it's healthy to jettison bad actors from your life or career, or to take sabbaticals from toxic people.

And as you consider adding a life partner to your portfolio, know that you are adding a permanent member to your team from a spiritual, financial, and wellness perspective. Mike and I try to have quarterly business meetings as a couple to discuss finances, life goals, family commitments, and health. It's okay to have a business element to your relationship, as you are all shareholders in a larger plan. I know many power couples hosting family business meetings while commuting home on the train out of Grand Central. They will each add items to the agenda from syncing childcare calendars and household finance concerns to managing families at the holidays.

When I want to buy a race car, Mike always takes me to the pre-owned section of the local Jeep dealership (we have had three Jeeps since getting married). My only vices are shoes, Weimaraner dogs, and nice red wine, the latter because bad wine gives me a migraine—and that goes against my message, even if I don't have data to prove it. So, while my work in PE is often about financial engineering or leverage, I have zero leverage in my personal life.

Along your journey, aspire to live below your means, because financial pressure can also make for poor health and add to the stresses you may already be experiencing during the climb. Remember that even after you make it. Yes, I hope you are well off as you read these words, but not for winning's sake. I got lucky—luck is when preparation meets opportunity, as Oprah often quotes. I spent a lifetime working on being prepared, and as a result, I haven't had a financial worry in decades and really don't need to work. But I *want* to work. There's a difference. Because where I am today is miles from where I started. Yet, it's a journey that I did not make entirely on my own. There are many people who helped me along the way.

IN RETROSPECT ...

Examine your education, experience, and network to determine what makes you qualified to be on someone's list. Also, create your own list, then look at the ratio of men to women or diverse candidates, including diversity of thought and life experiences. How can you work on your own qualifications to get on someone's list? Are you networking with a pipeline of leaders who will want to place you on their list? How can you develop someone else professionally so they can land on your list, or on someone else's list?

SECTION V
THE ADVOCATE

CHAPTER 6

BUILDING "TEAM MEG"

For the last few decades, I have built what I call "Team Meg," honest fans and brokers of my career who are there to offer me specific advice and coaching in areas where I'm weak and give me direct truth when I need it. For me, Team Meg is composed of people who have helped me in both my professional and personal life—people who have pushed and pulled me along and who have been there to celebrate my wins and to catch me when I've fallen.

Team Meg has been crucial for me in a male-dominated world of executives, where the reality is that males must help women break through the glass ceiling—something that's not discussed adequately in the executive woman's world but those in the know will quietly share when asked.

Today, in my classes, I ask my students to create their own team or board of directors and engage this group often.

During my ascent, I've had help from people that others often refer to as mentors. I've read articles debating the difference between mentors and sponsors, and I tend to prefer the latter term. To me, mentors give you advice on your path, choices at work, or presentation feedback. Sponsors are people who do shit for you. Sponsors are more like your own personal ambassadors. I've had the benefit of leaders who over time saw raw potential in me and, along with that, opportunities for me to potentially help the company or their division. They've put their necks on the line for me publicly—so in that regard, they've been ambassadors to my small country called Meg.

My sponsors could fill a pie chart: academic, professional, personal, and even the rare spot sponsors (short-term need) with the last of these being most difficult to have. What I've found with the majority of these sponsors is that it wasn't a matter of smashing the patriarchy; it was about working *within* it to get ahead.

ACADEMIC SPONSORS

Peter Arno and Michael Sparer helped shape my academic career in ways they will never know.

Peter Arno is a health economist and distinguished fellow at the City University of New York Institute for Health Equity. He wrote *Against the Odds: The Story of AIDS Drug Development, Politics and Profits*, which was nominated for a Pulitzer Prize. Peter has been instrumental in my success in three ways.

For starters, he introduced me to the research of Sir Michael

Gideon Marmot, which lit a candle in me around inequalities in health, including their causes and ways to mitigate them. Today, I find that at every meeting in healthcare we discuss his "status syndrome," which is how a patient's social standing directly affects his or her health and how socioeconomic position is an important determinant for health outcomes. I've personally witnessed this: I've seen patients miss appointments and not pick up medicine because they couldn't afford transportation. It's also why I ponder the use of livery cars or Uber when picking up an eighty-year-old, chronically ill patient. Why not use nursing or pharmacy students, who are trained in chronic care, and have the trip swing by their lab appointment and at a pharmacy to fill their prescriptions? Status syndrome continues to be a worthy area of debate, and I've often wondered if Health and Human Services should share a budget with urban planning and other divisions, such as education, to deal with a larger strategy to address socioeconomic status. A huge issue, no doubt, and one that I'm unsure will ever be solved in the US. I think trends and new business models addressing socioeconomic status will be an emerging and necessary field going forward. This would be a worthy White House appointment for a senior healthcare leader, especially in light of the opioid epidemic, gun violence, and the uninsured, which at their core are health issues with a social component.

Peter is also an intense editor and a beast to debate with. (I'm so glad he isn't editing this book.) He made me a better writer and insisted one of the first books I read on the subject be *On Writing Well: The Classic Guide to Writing Nonfiction* by William Zinsser. He knew that communication in academia and business is crucial for leaders—and others—and his insistence on excellence in this area was truly a gift.

Finally, Peter, along with Deborah Viola, PhD, a senior lecturer in the Department of Health Policy and Management at the School of Health Sciences and Practice at New York Medical College, literally dragged me across my doctorate dissertation finish line. Many doctoral candidates graduate "all but dissertation" (ABD) or remain a PhD(c) (candidate) for good reason. And some students don't make it because they implode during their oral argument, which I embarrassingly did. During my presentation, one committee member rightfully debated the use of household versus personal income in my findings and wondered why I chose one over the other. I was having none of it. After five years of study and two dissertation topics while still working a full-time job, I had zero time to entertain another data run or give the committee a proper answer. Well, the committee won. No diploma for me was the pending outcome.

As an aside: It has been a hard lesson for me to learn that not everything is a negotiation; sometimes whoever holds the power wins. One time, I tried to argue a traffic ticket with a George Washington Bridge tollbooth operator who said I was talking on my phone when I was wearing Beats headphones (cool looking but not regulation) and listening to something else. I sat for an hour on the side of the bridge arguing the point, but in the end, it didn't matter. He held all the cards and gave me an additional ticket for a broken turn signal. I had zero power and ultimately "negotiated" myself into a worse outcome.

After my dissertation circus, Peter called, exasperated, and shared that he would soon be leaving the department. So, as my committee chair, I had one chance to stick a water landing, he said, or I would basically have to start over. I reran my analysis, which did not have a material effect on my findings, and ultimately earned my doctorate. But it wasn't so much about attaining that distinction as it was about learning, once again the hard way, that it's not about winning; it's about getting what you want.

The other sponsor that helped shape me academically was Michael Sparer, whom I mentioned earlier as pushing me toward the teaching position at Columbia. Like Peter, Michael is a thought leader and brilliant leader in healthcare policy. While working toward my master's in public health at Columbia, I took Michael's popular class on healthcare systems around the world and was in awe that he could lecture for three hours like a storyteller—without the use of slides and with only a few notes. Years later, completely without reservation, I asked him to keynote at Cardinal Health's Strategy Day, where he spoke on the history of the ACA and all the policy events leading up to it. Of course, he left my business audience equally impressed.

Any time I have an academic idea, Columbia and Michael are right there to incubate it. Thanks to Michael (and Rebecca Sale, who runs the department and coined the "Business of Healthcare"), my class has so far been sponsored and renewed five years running.

PROFESSIONAL SPONSORS

I've had about ten meaningful roles in my career, and in those roles, most of my immediate bosses were men. It's not a value judgment, but more a reality of the times in which I ascended. I've also had a few high-profile female sponsors mentioned earlier, and two former Medco board members, whom I aspired to emulate and who then became my friends. Those Medco board members were Myrtle Potter, one of America's foremost healthcare leaders, and Nancy-Ann DeParle, who served as deputy chief of staff for policy in the Obama administration (among many other accolades on a long Wiki page). I continue to call all of these sponsors for career advice, content, and connections. They always call back, even as they continue to ascend. And Nancy-Ann, who is widely known for her brilliance and policy depth, is actually equal parts fun. Whenever there is a concert of interest in town, she is my go-to concert mate—we've seen U2, Peter Gabriel, and Sting.

In the last few years, I've been lucky to be included in two high-profile groups of women chaired by Christina Minnis, a senior leader at Goldman Sachs, and Barbara Ryan, a legend in biotech circles who started her own "Fab Pharma Females." Forget the dinners, events, and fun—these two have designed a system of mutual support and respect with a goal of advancing each other. This group of peers made it and many run or manage billions of dollars, so they are a higher form of "the list," where they vouch and help each other win big deals, get on Fortune 50 boards, and have an easy forum in which we can be ourselves. Each of them has helped me and has been in my corner on several deals. The results speak for themselves. And as a result of this group I became friends with two senior female PE partners, both who mentor and inspire me without reservation or concern for competition.

I wish there were more female CEOs and board members, as it would be way easier to GSD and relate. And I will leave this earth having minted more females into CEO and titans of the industry. What is common among my female peers mentioned is a genuine interest to do the same. At last count, I have nearly twenty senior female friends (close friends) in the industry running billions of dollars as CEOs, bankers, PE partners, and entrepreneurs. We help each other and share the same goal—to one day see more heels in the halls of power.

Still, when I think about my career through the lens of my largely male bosses, one thing is clear—I choose well. I've intuitively known how to pick bright stars, winners, and those dedicated to changing the complexion of the corner office. Winners are less likely to be micromanagers, threatened by you, or trying to dim your light. Winning leaders want you to climb and are even happy when you ascend above them. I often look for a small bit of me in any leader that I want to work for.

> **Winners are less likely to be micromanagers, threatened by you, or trying to dim your light. Winning leaders want you to climb and are even happy when you ascend above them.**

PERSONAL SPONSORS

My Team Meg also includes family members like my mom; my husband, Mike; my brother; my mother-in-law, Linda, who as a serendipitous bonus was a healthcare HR executive; and my assistant, Stephanie Kline, who runs my show. When I arrived at Cardinal Health, Stephanie was in executive recruitment, helping me and other executives onboard into the company. I needed an executive assistant and was desperate for a company insider whose connections and equity would help me assimilate. The next morning, Stephanie promised to do some recon and put a few confidential resumes in a red folder on my chair. When I opened the envelope, there was one CV: hers. I'll never forget it; she said, "You are going places and so am I." As I write this, we've been together nearly a decade and she runs Team Meg. She was the best hire of my life.

I also have an email and text group that is part of my morning read, jokingly known as the "Pharm," that has a few past colleagues. In that group, we debate what is currently going on in healthcare, the economy, and politics. It's a safe chain in which to debate and ask any question, propose a debate, or serve as a daily echo chamber of humor. We've debated whether Amazon was going to become a pharmacy, thoughts on new policies, and whether the #MeToo movement was having a negative effect on senior women. We might also share job prospects, pay, and references—all questions and topics that none of us would want to bring up with a boss or at a town hall but which we might need answers to in order to shape our thinking before going public. I never miss breaking healthcare news, because the Pharm ensures we cover each other's space with a byline.

Everyone needs the benefit of a diverse team personally—and professionally.

While you want people who are your allies, there must also be room for disagreement, because debate is healthy. I learn by debating, and that's something I recommend be learned early. Coming up the ladder, I found that many were put off by my debate style and it would show up in my yearly performance reviews as "Meg can be aggressive." Debate and taking different positions is how I learn, so I've had to alter my style to accommodate others. I learned to say ahead of time, "Let's scrimmage on this topic," which let the participants know it was a live debate. Similar to a ref telling a boxer, "Protect yourself at all times," those on my team became more comfortable with the format. When someone rejects your idea—which will happen at some point—you must condition yourself to defend your position with data, shoulders back and confident in your points. Over time, you won't need a beta-blocker, nor will you need to lose sleep dreading the board meeting or presentation—you'll be like a fish to water. I often hear people say, "It's not personal; it's business." That is largely true, but I've learned that temperament and delivery make a world of difference, whether the debate is in a personal or professional setting.

Finally, if you land hard on someone, apologize publicly. Let others know you are learning and care about how they feel. A big public apology or an admission that a lesson has been learned or a point ceded, especially from a senior leader, goes a long way and sets a great example.

"SPOT SPONSORS"

What is a "spot sponsor"? To be crude, it's a disposable connection for a specific request. For those readers who have been my spot sponsors, know the favor will be returned if not already.

Let's say you want to meet a high-profile leader like Salman Khan or are up for a coveted role on a high-profile board, and you find out that your next-door neighbor is friends with the CEO; maybe they sit on a community board together. Or maybe you're surfing LinkedIn and find someone you know well who is also connected to a few rock stars you'd love to know. Basically, you are one friend or colleague away from someone that you need for an important reason. This is basically part of LinkedIn's business model, but I'm taking it a step further in that you don't need a connection; you need action from this person now. Maybe you need that person to vouch for you, introduce you to a customer, serve as a character reference, give you diligence intel, or get you into a certain doctor or hospital. Sometimes, you need that one-off person to neutralize a threat; maybe you were on a nonperforming team and have a negative halo that needs some mitigation.

It can be a tough situation, because your cultivation time is likely low and can come off as incredibly fake and transparent. So, you will have to expend personal equity through someone else, a "connector," and get that person to use their equity to help you. This is why I wanted a well-connected assistant when joining Cardinal.

People call me a health connector and, jokingly, a "Kevin Bacon of healthcare" (that whole six degrees of separation thing). Since I've been in healthcare for twenty-plus years, I choose winning bosses, and I love to make smart friends, I'm often one phone call away from anyone in the space and that's a huge advantage to my friends. But for those who have reached out to me (sometimes as a spot sponsor), I often offer a reminder that it took twenty years for me to make the one phone call they are asking for. Are you worth it? You want me to call this Fortune 25 CEO for you; why would I do that for you? I can make that call once, maybe twice in an entire career.

> **Stay close to connectors. Make sure you are worthy of the ask, and express your gratitude afterward.**

Stay close to connectors. Make sure you are worthy of the ask, and express your gratitude afterward. I've had several people call me to serve as references to potential bosses in PE, people they didn't know but realized that I did. The problem is, I hadn't heard from some of these people in five years. Big mistake. Instead, identify people along your career journey who are likely to ascend, people who make companies run or public-policy people who are out influencing the debate and future of your industry. That also works in reverse; I've overconnected some of my friends. One called me recently and told me that they didn't have the capacity to look at another start-up right now. So, choose your spots carefully.

In a clutch, if you must call upon a distant acquaintance, be honest. "I'm sorry to be calling you, but I value your guidance or advice. I see that you know Meg and hope you don't mind that I called." When you are finished making the connection, immediately FedEx or mail a handwritten card thanking the person. They won't forget it. Right around the time I was writing this, I needed help with a family member stricken with a rare cancer; specifically, that person needed access to a medicine and medical advice. I used two close friends, who used their relationships to get me some spot sponsors, who went into action on my behalf. I knew this was a once-in-a-decade type of call, so everyone got a thank-you and a few folks got flowers. I was respectful and grateful for their time. And as result, my phone will be up one rung for them. Dr. Bruce Feinberg has been a connector for me on all things cancer. He is one of the most honest and well-read clinicians I know, and I never take his generosity for granted. And I am publicly thanking him here!

And genuine gratitude matters. Every Thanksgiving I call the five to ten people who helped me that year. I thank them specifically and wish them a happy few days off with their family. I'm grateful for them, and the call is right from the heart. And, at the holidays, I spend my own money on sending a small treat (cookies usually) to people who maybe didn't do something for me, but I'm still grateful for their friendship, or maybe they had a hard year and I want to give them a boost.

Don't wait until you need something to let people know you appreciate them. And if you get invited to a special group, industry event, or exclusive dinner, thank the host, even if it's an important partner like a banker. They chose to have you there versus your peer or competitor, so show some gratitude.

GETTING ON BOARDS

During my year off after leaving healthcare, I began working hard to join a few paying boards so that cash flowed, and professional momentum continued to wash over me. One thing I found to be true in that pursuit is the frustrating adage: "You can't get on a board until you are on a board." It's infuriating. On a similar note, I can remember talented folks at Merck or Pfizer not being able to get into marketing because they didn't "carry a bag" as a sales rep.

Recently, a high-profile female asked for my advice. She was offered a low-paying board as her first seat and wondered whether she should hold out. The criteria for your first board will be very different than your dream board, I told her. I asked her what was important to her. First, she liked the company and CEO. Next, she wanted something close to home geographically, because she still had kids in high school, and this opportunity was in close proximity. Then, she wanted something in her sector—the board was in the consumer sector, which fit her background as a marketer and would allow her to shine. Finally, she talked about the board composition, which was impressive. This last point really intrigued me because high-profile and established board members are the best network for getting on other boards—when they get inbound calls for boards, you can be in line to get their scraps. I remind my high-profile male board peers, please send your declines my way. Don't forget about me and my network.

When I chose my first board, Seniorlink, I wanted the seat because the company was mission driven around something that I really believed in. Seniorlink is using technology to transform care-giving in the home. I had been a caregiver in my teens; after my grandfather died, I often stayed with my grandmother to care for her because she had Alzheimer's. So, I understand the challenges that caregivers face, and I see technology as a way of helping this unher-alded workforce provide better quality care while reducing healthcare spending.

I met with Tom Riley, Seniorlink's CEO, at the famed J.P. Morgan Healthcare Conference in San Francisco, and absolutely fell in love with its model to serve caregivers in the home. Seniorlink had a high-profile board, but also had a top-flight management team, and as I write these words, I've been on that board for nearly five years and have gotten so much out of it.

Most of the boards—and people—I've chosen have been aligned with something that I care about from a value or healthcare perspective, something that is working to better the world.

However, everyone who wants to be on a board has a dream board that they aspire to be on. I aspired to be on a Fortune 200 healthcare board that had a progressive strategy to change the way healthcare is delivered. I was going for intellectual bragging rights.

One day, I got a call that Tenet Healthcare would be looking for a new board member and I might fit the bill. Tenet was mission driven—to help people live happier, healthier lives. And it had a powerful network of medical facilities, providing quality care to millions of patients through a wide range of services: from wellness and primary care to chronic-care management, urgent care, outpatient surgery, advanced diagnostics, rehabilitation, and acute hospital care.

And as a strategist, Tenet was forward looking. Under its adroit chairman and CEO, Ron Rittenmeyer, Tenet was focused on the part of healthcare most interesting to me at the time: integrated and comprehensive patient care. When it comes to managing populations of patients, many of whom will be covered at financial risk, it's important to cover and care for them wherever they reside—home, urgent care, outpatient surgery. The idea of "owning the patient" is overstated, because it's really about serving the patient in the best setting, and many vertical integration deals have focused on this premise. For instance, the merger of CVS and Aetna was designed to combine CVS Health's local presence and clinical capabilities with

Aetna's healthcare benefits and services in order to better integrate care and give consumers and their health providers more options for making informed decisions.[19]

For twenty years, I had been practicing what I would say in an interview for my dream board role. Senator Bob Kerrey was the lead director and helping to organize the search, and as I flew out to Tenet's headquarters in Dallas, Texas, I sat next to the senator on the plane. What I love about him, aside from his years of service, is his directness, which is probably well honed as an adept politician. As the plane reached altitude, Senator Kerrey spun around and said, "So, your competition is General Lloyd Austin III." *What?* It was as if we'd descended 10,000 feet and I needed an oxygen mask. General Austin (retired) served as twelfth commander of the US Central Command and was the thirty-third vice chief of staff of the US Army at Joint Base Myer-Henderson Hall, Virginia.

Instead of alarm, I realized how great that moment was, and it put me in flow. I had worked hard enough and long enough to be slotted against a general who had earned the Silver Star. I interviewed well and really felt Tenet would benefit from my entire career as a clinician, operator, and strategist. But I decided if I lost to the general, I would go down with my head held high. I was a badass for having made it that far—and other opportunities would come. In preparing for that role, I was able to lean on my network to understand what Tenet needed in a board member—once again, my friendlies served as a validating reference check, confirming I had the goods.

A month later, General Austin and I were mates in Tenet training together. The board took both of us. Since then, I have learned so

---

19   "CVS Health to Acquire Aetna; Combination to Provide Consumers with a Better Experience, Reduced Costs and Improved Access to Healthcare Experts in Homes and Communities Across the Country," *Cision PR Newswire*, December 3, 2017, accessed January 2, 2019, https://www.prnewswire.com/news-releases/cvs-health-to-acquire-aetna-combination-to-provide-consumers-with-a-better-experience-reduced-costs-and-improved-access-to-healthcare-experts-in-homes-and-communities-across-the-country-300565669.html.

much from General Austin, just by being around him, listening to his questions and experiences on leadership. (And my mom still gets a kick out of the press release where I'm featured after General Austin on my dream board.)

MINT YOUR OWN LEADERS

As I mentioned earlier, these days, I aspire to make other CEOs. But minting other leaders is something that I've believed in doing all along. Senior leaders have helped me along the way, and as a senior leader, I have that same responsibility. When you advance competent leaders, their ascent can take you even higher because it also scales your brand and reach. Anyone who has worked for me knows how much I value the patient, looking around corners, and a GSD mentality. It's hard to imagine those same traits aren't being amplified across their own companies.

When Tom Burke was my chief operating officer at Cardinal in the specialty division, he helped make me successful there, not to mention countless others. When he left Cardinal and became CEO of another company, he offered me a seat on his board. When that company was acquired, both of our boats ascended higher. I have a few colleagues who often say, "Let's get the band back together," meaning we trust one another, and the sum of our parts make for a stronger company.

As you ascend and amass your own content and connections, be ready to use them to help others—even those above you. All these bosses took chances on me and, in turn, I have worked hard to make them not regret the choice and continue to sponsor me. Pay it forward and today, more than ever, also pay it backward. I've helped place former sponsors on boards and always find a way to help them transition into academia, which is often a goal for talented leaders. I've given my "Business of Healthcare" syllabus to other leaders looking to teach for the first time. In addition, find junior leaders and shine some of your light on them. Ensure others who work for you do the same. Leaders underneath you are an annuity that pays off for years to come.

CHAPTER 7

YOUR HEALTH– PART OF THE COMPENSATION PACKAGE

As I mentioned in the introduction, I finally made the decision to value health as highly as compensation and other life choices and benefits. Health is a form of wealth and can be accumulated.

I don't really agree with the concept of having it all or balance in life. To help bring this point home, let's look at a theoretical framework taught in public health, which comes from noted psychologist Abraham H. Maslow, who developed a theory of basic human needs and how they build upon one another to achieve physical, social, and spiritual health and well-being. These were all traits I attempted to investigate and understand in my study of executive women. In Maslow's hierarchy of needs, the last level, called "self-actualization," is very important as you ascend in your career, because it travels linear with your own growth. It refers to fulfilling your individual potential, whether that means becoming a nurse or CEO or starting your own company.[20] Throughout my career, I often traded balance for driving toward my goals and ultimate contributions to my job, my life, and to others around me.

In order to get to a higher level of career or life goal, your basic health needs must be addressed so that they don't become a hindrance. That is why considering personal health throughout your career is paramount to your success. Whether it's having an on-site medical clinic, allowing employees to work remotely, letting them take a brief sabbatical, or making it possible for them to care for family members, the health quotient is part of the new compensation package. One of my best friends is proof of that: she landed a job at a company that allows her to work from home one day a week of her choosing. This new job also came with a 30 percent bump in pay, but that was the last part of the news she was so excited to share. She was over the moon about the one day of flexibility, because it would allow her to see her mom, who was recovering from cancer, without having to leave work early or take a day off or make her feel like she wasn't committed and without revealing her personal issue.

As an academic, I find the intersection of the caregiving crisis and executive health an interesting field of study, given that nearly three-fourths of workers in the US are also juggling caregiving

---

20   Ann Olson, "The Theory of Self-Actualization," *Psychology Today*, August 13, 2013, accessed February 20, 2019, https://www.psychologytoday.com/us/blog/theory-and-psychopathology/201308/the-theory-self-actualization.

responsibilities. One study found that nearly one-third of those workers (32 percent) left their jobs because they found it impossible to balance their responsibilities at work and at home. Some 28 percent of workers said that, because of caregiving, they were passed over for a raise, promotion, or challenging assignments at work. What's interesting is the discrepancy in viewpoints of the problem: a good portion of the workers in the study (80 percent) said they were unable to do their best work because of their caregiving roles, but only around one-quarter of employers (24 percent) reported that their employees' performance was affected.[21] As I mentioned earlier, women executives are masters of deception when it comes to the transitions between work and home. As long as someone isn't causing a safety issue, we need to support executive caregivers in the workplace and work through the transition with them, not around them. For a top performer, a career offers a needed distraction and is often one's identity—and companies need to recognize that the majority of their workforce will be caregivers and employees at the same time.

As an employee, do your part when it comes to your health—whether on the job or outside work. That means remembering to triage. Triaging is not something an employer can do for you. No one can take care of everyone or everything at once. So, you must triage what is in your power to take care of.

HEALTH: AS VALUABLE AS MONEY, TIME OFF, AND UPWARD MOBILITY

In the study I conducted, I found that the more women earn, the less healthy they feel. While women with more resources reported

---

21   David Harrison, "Employers Need to Address 'Caregiving Crisis,' Study Finds," *Wall Street Journal*, January 16, 2019, accessed February 2, 2019, https://www.wsj.com/articles/employers-need-to-address-caregiving-crisis-study-finds-11547636400.

being healthier and less stressed based on specific measures, they were worried about their health. I did not unearth the causal reasons for the discrepancy: maybe wealthier, more educated women have higher standards for their health, or have harsher standards and view themselves as falling short of their definition of ideal. Since they have higher levels of education, maybe they are simply more aware of what a sedate job, lack of sleep, too much stress, and too much alcohol can do to the body. And that raises their anxiety about their health. Maybe they are more focused on their health because they don't have other worries, such as how they are going to pay this month's utilities, mortgage, student loan, or other bills—maybe, without those financial concerns, they simply have more brain energy to devote to the state of their health.

Ever since I conducted the study and, in examining my own ascent, one thing has become crystal clear to me: no matter how much a person earns or how much education he or she has, health is a concern, even if only talked about privately. At a small dinner one year at the WEF in Davos, International Monetary Fund head Christine Lagarde talked about balancing life and work. All across the room, other powerful, accomplished women revealed that their daily lives were remarkably similar to lives of those hundreds of women that I had surveyed for my research. Everyone was technically working seven days a week. Some also had children to care for and many were also managing the care of elderly parents in a different time zone or across an ocean. No wonder self-care tends to take a back seat for so many women and, even for those with resources, it becomes something to add to the "worry-about" pile.

In previous chapters, I've mentioned how I felt like I could never call in sick during my ascent—even having to work on a laptop bedside while caring for my mom as she struggled to come out on the right side of a brain tumor. Many female colleagues—and respondents to my survey—have said the same thing. Any sick days taken are likely being used to take care of others.

That's why I believe that, while money is important in negotiating for a position—and you should always negotiate the best market package—your health should also be considered as part of your compensation package. Consider your health as a form of wealth in terms of math where possible. I used to say that on a $150,000 job, not commuting would be worth $25,000. The time I would get back would be equal to a bonus. Would being on a team that valued half-day Fridays in the summer, or had emergency day care, be worth $10,000 a year?

When negotiating or researching a potential job, do what you can to set it up as a healthy job from the start. For starters, consider company culture and leadership. Does the company back up the image it presents to the world? Cardinal was a health company, and as I mentioned, it had an on-site health clinic. It also had an on-site gym so people could scoot down and exercise after work or even over lunch (although, I think, as a woman, it's a little harder to get cleaned up after a workout, what with the hair and the makeup and all). Or, is it the kind of company where you show up to work in the dark, and leave in the dark, with nothing in the way of a healthy break all day long? Don't start a job and then two years later find that you've gained twenty pounds or only sleep a few nights a week, because you didn't build health into your schedule from the start. I've been to locations where all they had was a candy-vending machine—and I've been to others who gave free fruit. That small stuff adds up.

Look for companies whose health values align with your own. I would not work for a tobacco company, because that does not align with my views. Instead, I've always chosen companies where I like the brand and I believe they're doing well by doing good. They're solving some unmet need in healthcare. Merck and Pfizer were dedicated to bringing new medicines to the world.

I also tend to work with people who value their own health, which means that they're going to value my health and well-being. Many of my immediate bosses were happy and healthy people. One company cared that I lost my sister and was interested in how I was doing through that. Another boss cared about where I was living and that I had that long commute. In a meeting, a colleague covered my area while I went to the clinic for a migraine shot. I was on the Gelesis board because it addressed obesity. I'm on the Tenet board because it has a long history of working across the healthcare system to improve service delivery and patient outcomes. I'm on the Seniorlink board because it puts caregivers on the map and will leave a contribution to the world long after I'm gone. You can see a pattern to the products and people I work for.

Don't work for people who make you sick. Relocate from them quickly, even at a financial loss.

Don't work for people who make you sick. Relocate from them quickly, even at a financial loss. It took me a while to realize what flying to Ohio was doing to my health or that spending three hours a day on a train commuting to Pfizer was leaving me no time to exercise. These situations can go on for a while if you are investing in an ascent, but they can't go on for years if health is something you value.

According to the US Census Bureau, ninety-minute, one-way commutes are on the rise—that's more than thirty-one full days every year.[22] One full month on the road. Do you have that kind

22   Melanie A. Rapino and Alison K. Fields, "Mega Commuting in the U.S.," US Census Bureau, 2013, https://www.census.gov/library/working-papers/2013/demo/SEHSD-WP2013-03.html.

of commute? Do you commute two hours one way, as I did when I worked for Medco and had to traverse the Tappan Zee Bridge every day? If so, ask yourself *why*. Would you be willing to take $10,000 less as a tradeoff for that commute? What would you do with an extra two hours a day, if you could get them back?

When vetting a company, find out their policy for caregiving or if there are any work-at-home options. Even one afternoon a week can be huge for some people.

As you climb, keep finding ways to fit health into your day. At one place I worked, a group of people always went running over the lunch hour. A lot of people are measuring their steps now, trying to get in 10,000 per day. Sometimes I see groups setting up a walking meeting—they'll do their weekly update on a forty-five-minute walk. Others park at the far corners of the lot when they arrive at work, and then take the stairs instead of the elevator to their floor. I used to see one guy's vintage Jeep so far away from the entrance that it made me chuckle, because I knew exactly what he was up to and gave him a mental high five. One CEO told me that he measures his steps every day, and when he gets home, he finishes his steps off by taking his dog for a walk. There are so many ways to track your steps that it's incumbent upon you to figure a way to move your body. There is no job on Earth where you can't find a way to get steps in. And if you travel for work, see if your gym membership is good at other locations. I pack lightweight racing flats from my track days, so getting in a run is never an issue. These lightweight sneakers are permanently in my bag along with doubles of everything so that I don't have to repack, which eliminates a lot of stress.

When it comes to health, also watch what you eat and drink— admittedly a challenge at work functions. I love dessert, but monitor what I eat using the app MyFitnessPal; it lets me track the calories

I take and work off in a day. I also avoided drinking alcohol until I was in my thirties, as nothing good comes from a buzzed executive. Today, I still attend a lot of business dinners, so to keep from over-indulging when alcohol is being served, I'll try to order something I don't really like to drink, such as bad white wine. That way, I'll just sip it.

Also, don't discount the value of sleep. It's fair to say that less than six hours of sleep consistently is insufficient and unhealthy. A study by the Labor Department showed that women are working longer than ever and sleeping less, shrinking the gap between men and women.[23] When I worked at Pfizer, I used to run on empty all the time but would try to make up for it by sleeping like a hibernating bear on Saturdays until my friend woke me to ensure I was up and having a life. That's not the case today. I can no longer function without sleep—and I need eight consistent hours nowadays. I was also an early adopter of the air machine, adapted from using vacuums to put infants to sleep; in the 1990s, I would travel with my big Holmes air purifier to help hum me to sleep. Today, I can use a white noise app, and recently a friend sent Bose white-noise buds my way. Innovation has really progressed to help you manage sleep.

Health doesn't have to cost a lot. A Peloton exercise machine or trainer is great if you can afford it. But if you can't, there are thousands of free videos online—I know people who do exercises by watching videos on their phones. I got caught up in trying a handstand every day (when I heard Jeff Bezos was doing this) until I took out the elegant in-room bar cart in a Soho House. The irony wasn't lost on me. The bottom line is: What works for you? Do you prefer more

---

23   David Harrison and Soo Oh, "Women Working Longer Hours, Sleeping Less, as They Juggle Commitments," *The Wall Street Journal*, accessed June 24, 2019, https://www.wsj.com/articles/women-working-longer-hours-sleeping-less-labor-department-finds-11560980344.

regimented exercise? Do you need a trainer? Or are you more like me and prefer playing a sport and moving with someone who helps keep you accountable?

OUTSIDE WORK, FOCUS ON QUALITY, LESS ON QUANTITY

By now, you are likely tired of me sharing my challenge and dislike for the term "balance," as if putting your career or life into an "equal steady position so it doesn't fall" is possible? However, I do believe that you can control life outside work by having a focus on quality, less on quantity. When my dad died, a therapist told me that you can take sabbaticals from people and situations to help provide more time for you. In a world that is now finding the fine art of tidying up, you can do the same with relationships and outside-of-work commitments. Even though I was driven my entire career, I have managed to always maintain that outside quality on some level. If you are going to have a few free Saturday nights a month, they might as well be good ones. I have ten close girlfriends from childhood and have added a few more high-quality sisters (and brothers) along my climb.

I've had a lifelong love of sports, having grown up in a nearly all-boys neighborhood with my best friend, Krista, who remains my best friend to this day. Krista and I played pond ice hockey. It was a brutal sport, but certainly an indoctrination for life and the importance of teams. My superpower back then was that I could run— lightning fast. When the bus dropped us off after school, I could beat almost anyone to the pond (which solidified a chance to be an early pick) except for the wily Parham brothers who often ran to the pond with their skates on. It still makes me laugh to this day. At age five, I ran in my first 5K, a race held by my grammar school that also included mothers. I won my age group, only to find that no one else was in my age group—I was the only one standing there expecting a medal. When playing huge games of "town tag" that covered miles, no one—not even my dad in a station wagon—could catch me. The kids in the neighborhood called me a deer because of how fast and long I could run. Sometimes on weekends, I would run with my dad—that is, until he complained of pain in his side, which turned out to be the tumor that led to his demise.

I ran, in part, because it was inexpensive compared to another sport that I participated in: figure skating. I skated for many years at a rink that was next to the local dump—and the rink itself was dumpy. The ceiling had gaping holes and birds sat in the rafters shitting on skaters. Apparently, the actor Paul Newman learned to skate there for the movie *Slap Shot*, so it had some fame. The ice was cold and hard, which, for a skater, was pure magic. I complained incessantly about my feet, because I have self-diagnosed Raynaud's disease, so my limbs are always cold when I play in a winter sport. (Wherever I go, corporate boardrooms remind me of ice rinks—they seem to always be running at 60 degrees Fahrenheit; my nose is always running when I'm presenting, like being on a ski lift. At Cardinal, I snuck my own heater into the boardroom ahead of time.) I gave up figure skating after I mastered the axel—one of the more difficult jumps—and after I had attained all the badges in the sport—they covered both sleeves on my skating dress. So, I concentrated on running whenever possible. Fortunately, that earned me scholarship money to college, which we desperately needed after my dad died.

To me, there is a difference between sport and exercise. I like the competition and camaraderie of a sport and it can be done with colleagues. To be solo on an elliptical, mindlessly checking off forty minutes, is pure death to me. I would rather hike or be outside for twenty minutes or rent a bike in a foreign city. Running doesn't cost any money, and you can do it almost anywhere. It's about stamina, pace, and math—a great analogy for life.

After college, I tried every sport I could—I've never found a sport I didn't like or couldn't master at a basic level. At the dialysis clinic, I played on the company's softball team, which continued under a new name, the Asthmaniacs, when I left to join Merck to work on Singulair. I always played on any other group sport that the workplace supported—it was a great way to find new friends and bond with coworkers. When I was at Pfizer, spinning was starting to be a thing. My mom and I went spinning daily, and eventually we went to Johnny G's spin school, where we became spinning instructors. To this day, I can still hear the awful beat mix Mom played in her class.

While I was working at Medco, Mike and I got into training for triathlons. I could barely swim, so he coached me, but I still struggled with the transition between swimming and biking—I couldn't get the wet suit off. One time, I fell over, taking out a bunch of bikes with me. I moved on to snowboarding, which I found to be much more fun than skiing and similar to skating and surfing. While I was at Cardinal, I signed Mike up for jujitsu as a birthday gift, and we both became obsessed. The idea of playing chess on the floor with competitors bigger and stronger than me was exhilarating. I was out of control on the mats during our "rolls" (live simulation), earning the name "Meggie Machiney." One day, I let my competitive drive take over and flipped a guy (the only one in the academy who was also a straw weight) into the wall. That's when our renowned coach, Márcio Stambowsky, one of the original Gracies of the famous Brazilian martial artists and an eighth-degree (red and white) black belt, took me aside to discuss the idea of slowing down. *Jujitsu is a gentle sport*, he explained. So, I learned from jujitsu how powerful the body can be and how to keep it safe. I still know how to choke out a 185-pound male (which I did to a colleague at dinner recently) and feel confident in defending myself. Eventually, I moved on from jujitsu and started hot yoga with some other friends.

Also, while at Cardinal, the chief technology officer, Brent Stutz, asked if I wanted to join him in the New York City Marathon, indicating what fun it would be. We knew the sponsor, so we had a chance to get in if we ran for a cause—which was a no-brainer. Not being one to turn down a competitive bonding experience, I agreed. That was September, two months away from the marathon. But I got up to eighteen miles as a base (*do not* do this) and finished the marathon in five hours on the nose—off my goal of four hours by a pretty wide margin, but still, I finished. Training for a marathon with a colleague made us competitive together—though, unfortunately, he got an injury and couldn't make it on race day. Also, it made for some accountability and provided some opportunities to bond. If you can find an accountability partner at work, even if you can't train together, check in on each other or promise a prize at the end of your mutual goal.

Today, it's all about moving. I just find ways to move my body four times a week. I just ran the New York Marathon again this year for Team Debra (www.debra.org) and epidermolysis bullosa, the worst disease you've never heard of, but this time with three months' notice and a coach. I'm always moving on and I attempt to try a new sport or have a big goal every year. I have a sports shed at my house with everything you might like to try. And as I age, it's the weight training that gives the highest bang for effort. At a minimum, count your steps or try a thirty-second plank a day.

IN RETROSPECT ...

As you ascend, build your own "Team Meg," composed of career fans and brokers, people who will give you specific advice, coach you in weak areas, and be truthful when you need it. Make a list of people you consider to be sponsors. What traits do they have? In what ways have they helped you? Then, make a list of the traits that you have and ways that you can use them to mentor or sponsor others.

Identify people in your life that you currently sponsor, and then identify other candidates you feel would benefit from your sponsorship.

Most jobs will demand a lot of your time, so that time should be valuable to your larger life goals and be worth the journey. If you are doing well by others, sometimes you'll reach a level where work feels more like a vocation.

As you ascend, ask yourself whether the job you are in or are pursuing is the best fit. Are you proud to talk about this company, mission, and your role outside work? Does this job all in (commute, homework, travel) cost you more than seventy hours a week of your time? Is this role compatible with your health? Does the company have an on-site clinic and/or gym? Is it a good cultural and mental sanity fit? Will the stress levels allow you to get adequate sleep? Will the stress levels cause you migraines or lead to problems with alcohol abuse?

Here's something I used to tell my team: for one month straight, every day when you get home, give the day a one-to-ten score on the "joy" scale. Was today fun? If you average eight-plus, you are doing well. I've had positions that were fours, from which I quickly moved on.

Create a pie chart of your month or quarter that breaks down how you spend your life. If 20 percent of your time is on a plane, it might flag an issue.

CONCLUSION

BACK TO WHERE IT ALL STARTED

Believe it or not, I'm back to renewing my nursing license in the state of Florida. So far, that has meant taking a refresher course, including around 180 hours of didactic training. That's what it will take for me to be eligible to get my license back. And for me, it's a fun hobby as that is what education does for me. The more content the better.

But what really prompted this was a desire to give back and volunteer. There are many underserved areas that still have access and affordability challenges where I would be glad to help. Many of the guys who work on my house complain of having no insurance or having to pay cash whenever they are sick. For those of my friends in the gig economy, I'm often the one who helps them procure care or medicine. I feel that being on the front line as a volunteer even per diem would allow me to survey areas up close that need a new model or investment, which is what my job is as an investor—you are really a public-health detective. It's also why many of my investor physician friends keep their licenses up to date. Who better to invest in healthcare than a private-equity nurse? And I'm at a point in my career where contribution to my field and society weighs heavily on me.

After spending a few all-nighters rereading principles studied many years ago with great interest, I was struck most with the summary point of nursing: "The basic tenet of nursing is to determine the consumers' needs and wants in order to guide them through their health experience."[24] That, for me, is why the business of healthcare came relatively easily and enjoyably. I have always cared about and been interested in the patient, and I think *everyone* working in health-care, regardless of level, should read an intro to nursing and/or public health 101 book as a basis or primer for their work—because we can always learn more, we can always do more, and the best business solutions are those closest to the patient.

ENABLING INNOVATION

As someone who has always been interested in what's around the corner, I've also taken a step to enable the next generation of innovation in healthcare. As cofounder of the company K2 HealthVentures, launched in 2019, we provide debt and equity capital to venture- and growth-stage companies in the life-sciences and healthcare industries. We invest in life-science companies with the dual goals of profit

---

24   Linda Honan, *Focus on Adult Health: Medical-Surgical Nursing*, (Philadelphia: Lippincott Williams & Wilkins, 2013).

and purpose. Our team wants to help fuel the growth of life-sciences companies and the advancement of new treatment options, ultimately to improve the lives of patients. In fine public-health form, our team decided to put a percentage of the profits to underserved disease areas.

My goal now as an investor is to fund *important* things. I will continue to demonstrate that innovation should not be seen solely as a moonshot—although that is important—but it should be seen as a procedural innovation in getting patients to the lowest cost setting, addressing socioeconomic conditions, and miscellaneous things like getting medical bills paid are all worthy endeavors, even if they don't get sexy press releases. And if I had to guess what is next for me, it would be trying to start a fund with like-minded partners and leaders. I have truly found my passion in life, which is to build businesses, and as a result—in a small way—shape our healthcare system.

I hope we see more progression on the healthcare-leadership front that finds more diversity in all forms. And I'm also including diversity of thought. I think more businesspeople entering the government, as seen at the US Food and Drug Administration and Health and Human Services today, is a good thing. And it would go a long way to have public-health leaders as board members to add to the debate, dialogue, and products that companies launch.

It's also beyond obvious that there is opportunity to advance more women leading and starting companies in healthcare given their market power as the most powerful end buyers.

ASCEND YOUR OWN DAVOS

When I first began writing this book, I envisioned the title or a future article being called *Ascending Davos,* because it was one of many symbolic moments in my career journey. Not only was I an attendee; I was now invited to major events as a speaker. *And* maybe I had made it. But I also felt that way on my first day teaching the Business of Healthcare, getting into Columbia, finishing with top times in the 400-meter dash, eloping with Mike in Tahiti, launching a company like K2, and seeing my mom post–brain tumor jumping out of a plane. Being a board member or being asked to serve as senior adviser to a country's leadership are other examples. There are many peaks I channeled and envisioned that became a reality. And I can tie each of them back to education, preparation, and a fortress network.

So, attending Davos as a member was more of a metaphorical summit for me. It represented one of the many long-term goals I had envisioned—to be an executive, professor, and thought leader in healthcare. The ascension was the end product of many career tactics and numerous setbacks.

Everyone should envision a mountain or summit in your career. What is your Davos in life? What lies at the top of your personal peak? Is it graduating medical school? Is it becoming a CEO? Is it making a difference where you live? Is it becoming a parent? Do you want to make enough money that you can help make medical school tuition free? Set a goal. Fill in the blank: my Davos is _____. You may not know when it's going to hit, but have in your mind something that's a far enough climb that you can put in front of yourself— microgoals and longer goals to get you there. The view down on your climb is the real reward. You did it, so take a moment to relish it and share the success with those who helped you climb.

I've had two senior sponsors (and now good friends) recently step down from very prominent Fortune 500 CEO posts, and it's likely a hard change for them given the heights they'd reached. I've advised them to pause and take in the view. They changed the course of patient care for the better, created an enormous amount of shareholder value, and left thousands of employees better off as a result of their leadership, not to mention the groups of people like me who have ascended because of their sponsorship.

If you think of your career as a snowy mountain that must be ascended, you can understand that there will be near-miss avalanches and bad weather that must be traversed along the way. You may even get momentarily sidetracked, take a big snowball to the eye, and spend time at a base camp sucking on oxygen. Even if the idea of ascending a summit is cloudy in your mind, think of the ascent in terms of LSD—long, slow, distance. That's a concept my husband introduced me to when we were training for a triathlon. LSD helps to build a base. At the time, it was a foreign concept to me—in sports and in life—but it's one that I have come to appreciate as I ascend new mountains.

My journey from a hospital emergency room, through an important pit stop in the dusty desert of Tucson, and finally ascending to the most elusive halls of power of healthcare and business, is nothing short of surprising for those who knew me as an unbridled child. But with education, carefully curated experiences, a combination of content and connections, and a myopic focus on my GSD brand, I've found that anything is possible.

I hope this book and my story inspire you to prioritize your health as you climb the corporate ladder. I hope you've learned some lessons in these pages that you can apply to your own life and work. My final advice to you: make sure your journey is one in good health, and that those lucky enough to join you on it value health, as it will be your life's greatest gift.

ABOUT THE AUTHOR

Meghan FitzGerald is a professor, private-equity partner, and public-health leader with more than twenty years of clinical, strategic, and operating experience ascending the halls of corporate America. She is a managing partner at LetterOne, Private Equity, a firm with about $25 billion of capital under management. Meg leads L1 Health's healthcare investment strategy. Prior to entering private equity, Meg was at Cardinal Health in roles of executive vice president of strategy, mergers and acquisitions, and health policy and president of Cardinal Health Specialty Solutions. Before joining Cardinal Health, FitzGerald was senior vice president of the new markets international division and business development at Medco Health Solutions, Inc. She also held positions of increasing responsibility at Pfizer Global Pharmaceuticals and was in marketing at Merck and Sanofi-Synthélabo. She is a member of the boards of directors for Tenet Health, Seniorlink, ABB Optical, and K2 HealthVentures. She also conducted a groundbreaking study on the health of executive women, the results of which were reported in *Harvard Business Review* as "The More Women Earn, the Less Healthy They Feel." She coauthored "Longevity in the Workplace: 60 Is the New 40."

Meg has worked in nearly every sector of healthcare and is an expert speaker on the "Business of Healthcare," which is the class she teaches as an adjunct associate professor at Columbia University's Mailman School of Public Health in the Policy Department.

A lifelong athlete, Meg has been a runner since age five and today participates in adventure sports, including triathlons, snowboarding, and scuba diving. She is a die-hard New York Rangers and UFC fan and owner of rescue Weimaraners, who are her "Grey Ghosts." She is married to Wall Street macrostrategist Michael Darda. They reside in Naples, Florida, and Martha's Vineyard, Massachusetts.

ACKNOWLEDGMENTS

The following people deserve credit for their contribution to the climb and this book. First, you are nothing without good health, so Dr. Staw, thank you for being a lifelong health partner and great diagnostician and for keeping my asthma and migraines in check during the climb. My academic sponsors Peter Arno, Michael Sparer, Deborah Viola, Rebecca Sale, Columbia University School of Public Health, and Fairfield University School of Nursing for inspiring health to be my calling, career, and the reason for this story. The students I teach have been my life's greatest privilege and gift.

Thanks to the team at Advantage and ForbesBooks, including Regina, Nate, Kristin, and Jamie for steering me through this storytelling process. And to Linda Kauffman, Krysta Butler, James Bierman, and Jason Friesen for reviewing early drafts.

The climb through corporate America was tough, a big pivot, and nothing short of kismet for a nurse aspiring to transition into business. The following individuals took the rare and risky chance to either hire me directly or help put me in the game while still coaching from the sidelines. Some may be out of touch but are never out of my debt: Coach Joe Fisher, Enrique Hernandez, Cindy Barnard, Kathryn Grundhoeffer, Paul Enright, Sue Bokhari, Bill Meury, Holly Crosbie-Foote, Jonathan White, Alan Kessman, Howard Johnson, John Driscoll, Mike Kaufmann, and Karen Katen.

While in corporate America and then in private equity there were countless partners and team members who commiserated in my daily performance, ran interference, and were brave enough to call me out or prop me up when needed: Susan Stretesky, Jen and Lance Tyler, The Pfizer Strategy and COX-2 lifecycle team, Mike Myers, the entire "10x16" Specialty Team at Cardinal Health, Jon Levy, Nash Lalwani, Ivan Zhivago, Nicole Zairova, David and Leslie Lawrence, Elisabeth Svensson, Barbara Ryan, Justin Simoncini, Ritesh Shah, Katie Baron, Michael Rimland, Tim Van Biesen, Alyse Forcellina, Barbara Ryan, Suzanne Maselli, my founding partners at K2 HealthVentures, Dr. Bruce Feinberg, and the priceless Stephanie Kline, who remains a permanent gust of wind at my back.

All it takes is one person in power to help change your career trajectory. The following supersponsors put their own reputations on the line to advance my candidacy on boards, panels, and special invites and to open the ironclad doors that halt ascensions: George Barrett, Peter Neupert, Myrtle Potter, Nancy-Ann DeParle, Dave King, Dr. Derek Yach, Iris Bohnet, Tom Riley, Dan Welch, Byron Hemsley, Maureen Regan, John Koski, Rob Lowe, Daphne Zohar, John LaMattina, Rolf Classon, Franz Humer, Christina Minnis, Ron Rittenmeyer, Senator Bob Kerrey, General Lloyd Austin, Tom Burke, Deneen Howell, Ravi Sachdev, David Gluckman, Lou Shapiro, and LetterOne for attracting me to private equity.

To Wayne Mones, my high school guidance counselor; the Brien McMahon track coaches; and my forty-year-strong girl squad, who deserve their own line of thanks, as high school was a messy climb.

By and large, the journey all starts and ends with my family. The most influential force in life is my "ride or die" mom, Nancy, who has traveled the world with me and has been pushing my bum up every single rung of this ladder; my brilliant and patient husband, Mike, who has given me the gift of life; my special spirited brother Scott; and my Oma. The love and support from the Lynch family, Linda and Gary Knudtson, the "PEG" Fritsch, my godmother and G-girl Marge McCarthy, Paul Darda and the Darda Family, Krista Karvoski, Krissy Feuerhake, Ethelle Shatz, Martha Sierra, Erin Leighton, and the Brackman, Shore, and Siano families are beyond special gifts to my life.

The early losses of my dad (my first Mike) and sister (Kiera) were painfully replaced with an insatiable desire to bring some good to this world, and I hope they would be proud.

Finally, owning a dog (or another pet) is linked to improved health, and my three gray ghosts, Bauer, Hailey, and Claus, are evidence of that. Now go adopt a dog.

All my proceeds from this book, no matter how small, will be donated to Geoffrey Canada and the Harlem Children's Zone (hcz.org). Geoff spoke at my Columbia graduation, and I sat there in the audience feeling so inspired and honestly a little lazy. He gave me an anonymous gift of inspiration and now I'm paying it back and forward. His organization has the heart and math to prove my biggest lesson in life: education is the great equalizer.